CONTENTS

FOREWORD

Perspective is one of the great advantages of getting older. Evaluated experiences lead to valuable insights, which allow you to form a greater understanding of the world. This is how we grow.

A new mentoring relationship helps us to see something we couldn't discover on our own. A challenging problem forces us to reconsider our standard approach. A great book inspires us to look at our lives and make meaningful changes.

These moments are a gift—especially in today's world, where we're surrounded by ever-increasing noise.

Life has always been filled with change, but it's never happened as often or as quickly as it does now. Marketing content and loud opinions have always clamored for our attention but never at this rate or through so many different mediums.

When a leader finds something truly valuable, it makes its way to the front of the line. It goes on the top of their stack of books. They can't stop talking about it with the people in their lives. They want others to experience the benefit they've received.

The gap between this kind of excitement and genuine life change is a clear plan. There have to be executable steps. It's not enough to get the information—you must know what to do with it. This requires both internal drive and a strong support system.

This is what transforms a brilliant game plan into a winning outcome. This is what I admire about this book you're holding in your hands. I've given my life to leadership—I know the excitement that results from inspiring principles and compelling ideas. I've seen it firsthand in boardrooms, auditoriums, classrooms, and churches all over the world.

Closing the gap between information and action is challenging in every setting, but this is especially difficult for men in the church. They know they're supposed to participate, but they don't know what to do.

They know what to do at work; they know what to do in the gym; they know what to do when they're spending the weekend on their hobbies—but they desperately need practical help in matters of life and faith.

As coaches, our job is to prepare and inspire people to succeed in whatever they set their hands to.

I first met Jeff Little when he was a young leader at a pastors' event. He was eager to learn and grow in his leadership. Through serving his church and working practically to develop leaders, he's developed insights and proven practical steps that have had a lasting effect on the lives of many men.

Now, he's taking this next step by providing us with clear and practical insights that can make a significant impact on those you influence.

Life is not a game, but I do believe it's possible to win in life.

Not because you're making someone else lose but because you're competing with yourself to become the best version of who you are. You're reaching your maximum potential and experiencing the life God created you to live.

John Maxwell

Introduction

**THE GREATEST THING ABOUT SPORTS IS YOU PLAY TO WIN
THE GAME . . . WHEN YOU START TELLIN' ME IT DOESN'T
MATTER, THEN RETIRE. GET OUT!
— HERM EDWARDS**

*Don't you realize that in a race everyone runs,
but only one person gets the prize? So run to win!*
1 Corinthians 9:24 NLT

I love to compete.

I love to work hard and give my absolute best effort toward a worthy cause. I believe competition is always more meaningful in the context of a team. Independent of the final score, there's incredible value in the process.

It reveals your ability to respond to pressure and adversity.
It forces you to confront your weaknesses.
It provides opportunities for growth.
It can forge strong bonds of team chemistry.

But Herm Edwards and the apostle Paul were both right—it's not just about the journey. In the end, you play to win.

But what happens when you don't know the rules?
How can you win if you can't see the scoreboard?
What if your teammates understand even less than you do?

All of these scenarios are incredibly frustrating. I know this because I've experienced them firsthand.

When my oldest daughter was five years old, she joined a youth soccer league. They were looking for a coach. I knew "futbol" was the most popular sport in the world, but I didn't know the rules. It wasn't part of my East Texas upbringing. But I wanted to help the girls, so I agreed to jump in and coach.

They knew even less than I did.

It quickly became apparent they were far more interested in taking pictures, eating halftime snacks, and chasing butterflies than they were about soccer.

I started to lose it. The message was not registering. It wasn't getting through. So, I talked slower. I tried to make it as simple as possible:

> *This is a ball. The goal is to prevent the other team from kicking the ball in our goal and to kick the ball into their goal.*
>
> *Now repeat it back to me. What's the goal?*
> *What? No. It's not time to go to the bathroom.*
>
> *Let's get in a line and each take a turn kicking the ball in the goal. Got it? Good.*
> *Come back—you don't have a ball.*

You get the idea. It was more than a little frustrating.

Eventually, the lightbulb went on, and the girls understood what they were trying to do. By the end of the year, each of them had scored a goal. They were proud of what they accomplished. They knew the objective, they grew in their ability, and they made clear progress in their development.

At this point, you're probably wondering, *What does this have to do with me?*

Great question.

I'm not just a former soccer coach; I'm also a pastor. I've worked with men for decades. And let's just say, little girls aren't the only ones who get distracted by things that don't matter.

Here's why this is so important: There may not be a lot of scoring in soccer, but at least the rules are clearly defined. We can all see the scoreboard. We know what has to happen in order to win.

This explains why men often struggle with church. It seems more like chasing butterflies than putting the ball into the net and bringing home the championship trophy.

Over the years, I've tried all kinds of programs designed to reach men, from pancake breakfasts to themed weekend retreats. The lasting impact was often underwhelming because real life didn't create many opportunities for them to apply the things they were talking about.

They were willing to receive coaching and help in the spiritual areas of their lives, but most of them had no idea how to honestly evaluate their progress or to connect the dots between the Bible and what they did every day.

So, we got rid of all of our programs and started from scratch. In order to help them win, men needed to understand what they were trying to do. The goal wasn't the transfer of information. The goal wasn't another program or meeting in their already busy schedule.

The goal was to help them win in the areas of life they cared about the most.

We looked at the kinds of things men needed to be successful:

- What caused them to feel like they weren't winning at home?
- How could we help them honestly assess their level of maturity?
- Could they be developed in their professional careers through a greater understanding of God's Word?
- Was it possible to maintain integrity with their finances, stay faithful in their marriage, and train each of their children to have a genuine relationship with God?

- What would it take to make spiritual concepts and principles make sense to them in a tangible way?
- How could we help them measure their progress?
- What areas of their lives were underdeveloped because they'd never been coached?

Most of the men we worked with had considerable success in one area of their lives. Depending on which scoreboard they were looking at, they felt like a winner. The problem was—like most of us—they tended to spend all their time and energy where they were winning at the expense of the more challenging areas.

WE WANTED TO MAKE THEM RICH WHERE THEY WERE POOR.

We wanted to show them the way to win.

When the NFL season is over, only one team has won the Super Bowl. We recognize them because they're given the privilege of lifting the Lombardi Trophy, named after the winning head coach of the first Super Bowl and one of the most influential leaders in the history of sports.

Vince Lombardi said, "Winning is a habit. Unfortunately, so is losing."[1]

In other words, winning and losing are not random or arbitrary. There are things winners and losers do that directly contribute to the outcome.

Before we go any further, I want to clarify a few things.

First, life is not a game. However, on multiple occasions, the Bible uses competitive sports metaphors to demonstrate the discipline and training necessary to grow and become everything God created you to be.

We can't work or earn our way into a relationship with God. It can only be received as a gift. But once we've received this gift, we can apply the same effort and training an athlete uses to make the most out of their God-given ability. This is a critical distinction.

The things we care about most—our identity, our purpose, our relationship with our wife and our kids—are far more important than a game. We have to learn how to win in these areas. The earliest followers of Christ were known as "the Way" because of the distinct way they walked with God. This is *the Way* we're after.

Second, a relationship with God or a commitment to the Christian life does not mean you're always going to win. Life is filled with challenges, adversity, loss, grief, and all kinds of pain. Each of these provides the opportunity to develop our character. This is why James 1:2-3 tells us to consider it pure joy whenever we face trials. It's not the trials—it's what the trials produce in us.

The Way to Win is not a fail-proof formula to avoid loss. It's a journey to a deeper relationship with God. And yet, Jesus Himself promised to produce fruit (growth) in our lives as we walk with Him.

Very few of us would choose losing over winning, but there are more opportunities to learn and grow from our failures than from our successes. In other words, there is no losing. There's only winning or learning.

Third, our competition is not with our neighbors, our co-workers, our friends, our siblings, our parents, or anyone else. Our competition is with our own selfish nature, our fear, our pride, the ungodly influences of cultural narratives that don't agree with God's Word, and anything else that contributes to our unwillingness to become the person God created us to be.

And finally, we're not looking to make anyone else lose in order to make ourselves win. In fact, it's not even about us. As we'll soon discover, the way to win comes through putting the goals and the needs of the team above your own.

In fact, the highest level of winning isn't about you; it's about helping someone else win. You don't have to hit the game-winning shot to be a champion. These moments are only possible because of the unseen contribution of teammates who worked hard and did their part at practice, in the film room, developing a game plan, and from the bench.

I have three daughters and a son, so I didn't just coach soccer. I coached my son in American football—the kind I grew up with, that gives men the opportunity to exert their will every play along the line of scrimmage.

One day, a young man came out to join the team. He'd never played before. His mom brought him out to the field and kindly informed the coaches he was going to be the quarterback. We told her we were willing to coach her son, but like everyone else on the team, he did not have the right to choose his own position.

If every member of the team gives maximum effort and takes responsibility to offer their gifts and abilities for the sake of the team, the outcomes are extraordinary. This holds true in both football and life.

Ephesians 4:16 says that when God's people are connected to Jesus, they grow and become more loving as each person does their part.

This book has been designed for the context of a team. It's not a class or a program. It's not about the transfer of information. It's not a life hack, a TED talk, or a how-to video on YouTube. It's less about knowing and more about becoming.

It's designed to be experienced in the context of relationships. There are 38 chapters broken down into five unique sections. The chapters build on one another.

Some of you may be reading this on your own—don't hear what I'm not saying. I believe you will still benefit greatly from this process.

Even if you're studying this on your own, don't keep it to yourself. Along the way, talk about the things that stand out to you with the people closest to you (a friend, your spouse, or a roommate). This is how we change—not just what we think but how we actually live.

Think of it like a playbook, or a manual for scaling a mountain. The information is valuable, but having someone to walk you through it and apply it to your life is transformational.

I've seen it happen over and over. A group of guys start as strangers and end up as a team. Lifelong friendships are formed. Families are transformed. Businesses are revitalized. Churches are strengthened. Cultures are changed.

My prayer for you is that you'll experience this same development in the areas of life you care about the most. I'm praying for you, standing with you, and cheering you on.

The Winning Lifestyle

Personal Development

1

I Want More for You Than from You

What is the first thing that comes to your mind when someone asks, "How have you been?"

Most of us respond with some form of "busy," "crazy," or we say nothing because we're stuck trying to find a place to begin describing all the things we're juggling. It also makes us feel important. And most guys compete at nearly everything, so we like the idea that we're doing more than most.

We tell people we're busy because we *are* busy.

I can't think of one responsible, mature man who is sitting around waiting for something to do. Maybe they're out there, but I've never met them.

I know hundreds of men who are working hard, being responsible, building their career/business, while trying to lead their family, invest in their children, eat well and exercise regularly, grow spiritually, and check off the items on their bucket list.

These guys can't seem to find the time to do everything they're passionate about. I know these kinds of men because I am one.

There have been times at the end of a frantic day when I've thought, *I'll sleep when I'm dead.* You probably don't say it out loud, but you've at least thought it.

The last thing we need is another unproductive distraction on the schedule. Between career demands, family calendars, and the time left to chase our dreams, no one wants another vague meeting invite popping up on their phone.

From the time we wake up in the morning until we go to sleep at night, somebody wants something from us. Every day we're inundated with thousands of requests for attention, and marketers are getting bolder and more intrusive as this battle intensifies.

Time is a limited resource—and we all get the same amount every day. If we're really honest, some of us do more with it than others. But every one of us can learn to be more productive and intentional with the time we have.

Your time is one of the most valuable resources you've been given, and I want to both honor and respect your time. Life is too short to waste time, kill time, or spend time on things that don't matter.

What we all want is to invest our time—to intentionally direct it toward experiences that produce dividends and compound interest in our lives.

This sounds obvious, but it amazes me how easy it is to miss.

Without careful consideration, even the most committed among us can live at the mercy of deadlines and meeting notifications while missing out on the very things capable of producing the results we're truly longing for.

But once you begin to experience the benefits of consistent obedience and prioritizing wise decisions, you won't give it up. You'll move other things out of the way.

When we find something valuable that helps us accomplish the things that matter most, we don't let go of it.

This is the idea behind the approach of this book.

Our culture perpetuates the idea of the self-made man—the strong, silent loner who overcomes every obstacle to change the world, from John Wayne in the Wild West to John McClane taking down Hans Gruber in *Die Hard*.

Heroes don't need help—a real man is strong enough to take on the whole world by himself. Maybe this works in action movies, but real life doesn't usually work this way.

You don't have to do this alone.

By the second chapter of the Bible, God tells the first man that it's not good for him to be alone. This applies to more than finding a wife. We're made for relationships, a band of brothers, a team where we can accomplish far more together than we could on our own.

SUPERSTARS BREAK RECORDS, BUT TEAMS WIN CHAMPIONSHIPS.

Barry Sanders was the greatest running back I've ever seen, but he never won a championship.

Charles Barkley was a superstar in three different cities, but his greatest joy was the summer he spent winning Olympic gold with the Dream Team.

It's true in business. Steve Jobs was a genius, but he needed Steve Wozniak to build Apple. Bill Gates would not have achieved his success without the teamwork of Paul Allen and others. The idea of a single genius may sell books, but, with very few exceptions, it's simply not true.

This kind of greatness isn't built in a day. Anything worth doing takes time. Research and science show that the single greatest determining factor of personal development is whether the person believes they can and will grow.

Experts call this the growth mindset.[2] This is a great starting place, but I don't think we have to stop there.

You can manage your weaknesses. You can develop your strengths. And most important of all, you can become the person God created you to be. But you can't do it alone.

I've been around long enough to observe, experience, and attempt most of the ways that churches have tried to engage men.

Programs and strategies change—pancake breakfasts, themed retreats, sports leagues, service projects, Bible studies, book clubs, etc. Let me be clear: I'm deeply grateful and respect anyone who tries to serve others, make disciples, and add value to men.

I created this book to be a give, not a take. This is not another box to check on your to-do list. I'm not trying to get something from you—I want to add value to you.

This isn't about trying harder to be spiritual. It's not about giving back. It's not about philanthropy or trying to be a good person.

I know if men will become who God created them to be, in the long run they'll experience fulfillment in their souls, their families will benefit, their companies will be more successful, their neighborhoods will improve, and the world will be different.

God is supremely generous. When He asks us to do something, He always has our greatest good in mind—even when we can't see it.

This is the reason you were created. This is winning in life. This is what you're going to care about when you come to the end of your life and wonder, *Did my life matter?*

I believe many men are frustrated with their spiritual lives because they've lost sight of Jesus' original goal. They've confused the pursuit of historical, cultural, or traditional information with the simple day-to-day life with Jesus. It goes beyond Sunday morning to impact who we are every day.

One approach prepares you to take a test on doctrine and historical facts about our faith; the other shows you how to practically love and serve your family, develop your character, influence those around you, and make disciples.

They're not the same thing.

We understand development when it comes to sports, our careers, our hobbies, and even our personal lives. There are tangible goals we can shoot for. And yet, when it comes to our spiritual lives, it often feels more elusive.

The biblical word for development is "discipleship." And in the mind of Jesus, it wasn't nebulous or esoteric. It was clear. Disciples pick up their cross, lay down their lives, love God, serve others, and build the Kingdom. It's more than a class and the collection of information. It's an invitation to a different way of living.

We're not just going to read about it, think about it, and talk about it—we're actually going to do it.

Jesus is really smart. The incredible thing about this approach is that the benefits aren't confined to one area of your life. Becoming a better follower of Jesus is so much bigger than understanding what the preacher is talking about during a church service.

Spiritual development strengthens your soul. It forms you into the kind of man your wife is looking for, equips you as a father, strengthens the relationships with the other men in your life, and even produces servant leadership, which often results in promotion and career advancement.

You can do this—not because you're perfect, come from the right background, or have all the answers. All you need to be is willing. If you'll commit and agree to follow even when it gets difficult, you can experience it for yourself.

Discussion Questions

1. What has been the greatest obstacle to development in your life?

2. Name one area you want to develop either in your professional life, as a husband, or as a father.

3. Would having trusted friends help make an impact in your development? How?

Leadership Challenge

— Make the group meetings a priority.
— Do the reading and participate in the discussion.
— Get to know the guys in the group.

2

Everyone Needs a Coach

What do you think of when you hear the word "coach"?

Maybe you think of a fiery motivator like Vince Lombardi. Maybe you think of a wise teacher like Coach K or John Wooden. Maybe you think of a brilliant tactician like Bill Walsh or Bill Belichick. Maybe you imagine one of the young superstars like Sean McVay, Brad Stevens, or Dabo Swinney.

Or maybe you think of a guy with a belly and short shorts who reluctantly taught P.E.

No matter what they look like, their preferred coaching methods, or the subject they teach, every great coach shares one thing in common: They help you reach a level of performance you could not have achieved on your own.

- Great coaches see beyond what you are to what you could be.
- Great coaches challenge your thinking and test your will.
- Great coaches build disciplines to transform potential into ability.
- Great coaches don't allow you to ignore reality—they confront you with the truth.
- Great coaches understand that attitude and effort are more important than immediate outcomes.

Each of these statements remains true whether you're playing a sport, balancing a budget, running a marathon, preparing a presentation, preaching, parenting, or developing your life plan.

No one does anything truly worthwhile by themselves. On your own, you won't come close to the heights you're capable of.

NO ONE REACHES THEIR MAXIMUM POTENTIAL IN ANY AREA OF THEIR LIVES WITHOUT A COACH.

If you stop and think about it, the function of a coach is very similar to that of a parent, mentor, leader, and even pastor. Inherent in each of these roles is a passion to develop, to guide, to prepare, and to equip those in their care to become the absolute best possible versions of themselves.

They don't just give us information; they model for us what success looks like. Modeling is the highest form of teaching.

You might be thinking, *Okay, Jeff, you made your case. But if this is so valuable, why don't more people benefit from coaching?*

This is a great question—and it's also the driving force behind this book.

There are at least three primary reasons why more men don't experience the benefit of coaching:

1. We feel bad about asking for help.

There's this thing on the inside of every man—you can call it drive, pride, or ego—that is determined to prove he's strong, powerful, and significant. We want to win, we want to demonstrate our value, and we want to succeed on the basis of our talents, abilities, and hard work.

What's fascinating to me is that the same guy has no problem finding help for the people he cares about.

If you're a parent and your child needed help, most of you would do whatever you had to in order to get your child the help they needed. But somehow when it comes to your own developmental needs, it feels like weakness to admit you've hit a wall.

I want to give you permission to invest in yourself. If you're going to reach your maximum potential and become the man God created you to be, you need coaching.

The personal coaching industry has exploded in recent years because the results of this approach are difficult to ignore. In fact, development experts say a key determining factor is embracing a "growth mindset"— the internal conviction that you can and will improve your brain's capacity to learn and solve problems.

2. We don't think it applies to spiritual things.

It may be hard for us to admit we need it, but we understand the value of coaching in certain areas of our lives.

- **Do you want to get the most out of your physical health?** You'll need a coach to help you develop consistent workouts and to give you input on your diet and nutrition.
- **Do you want to advance in your career and build your professional skills?** You'll need a coach who's aware of best practices and proven strategies for growth.
- **What about your finances? Your marriage? Your parenting? Your favorite hobbies?** You'll need a coach who has already

helped others overcome the challenges waiting for you down the road in each of these areas.

But when it comes to their spiritual lives—how they relate to God, how they cultivate His presence and peace in their home, how they step out and lead their family in faith—most men think they're on their own. If there's help out there for these issues, most guys don't know where to find it.

If anyone should embrace a growth mindset, it's followers of Christ. The idea that each of us can be transformed into the person God created us to be comes right out of Scripture.[3] As valuable as coaching can be in the natural, day-to-day areas of life, it's even more valuable in the spiritual, eternal aspects of life.

Before I was a pastor, I had one. Even now, I have several of them. I'm also grateful for coaches and mentors who challenge me to grow into the person God created me to be. I hold their coaching in the highest esteem. I know the value it has provided in my life.

3. We're not "coachable."

We've all seen the super-talented athlete or young leader with incredible potential. Their problem is their attitude. They view input from a coach as insignificant, a necessary evil, or an obstacle to overcome.

People have always had challenges with authority. It may be more difficult today than ever before because, in our culture, we have unprecedented access to information. In previous generations, you had to go to an older authority figure—a parent, a teacher, or a boss. Now you can go straight to Google or YouTube and tell yourself you don't need anyone else.

Coachable people don't receive correction or coaching as criticism or rejection. They take it for what it truly is: invaluable wisdom. People who are insecure are defensive—they deflect criticism, they always have a reason why it's someone else's fault, and eventually, they even mock the person who's trying to help them get better.

"DO NOT REBUKE MOCKERS OR THEY WILL HATE YOU; REBUKE THE WISE AND THEY WILL LOVE YOU" (PROVERBS 9:8).

Don't be defensive. Don't make excuses. Predetermine to empower your coach to be honest with you.

The Bible has a word for someone who receives correction with gratitude and makes the necessary changes: *disciple.* Jesus loved the crowds, but He trained His disciples.

I was never the best athlete on any team I played on, but I realized that one of the easiest ways to give myself a competitive advantage was to become coachable. I would listen to feedback. I would implement what I was learning. I would try my best not to argue, get defensive, or push back out of stubbornness or pride.

I realized that being coachable wasn't dependent on how good my coach was. It was entirely up to me. And it could make up for a gap in talent or natural ability.

Some people are easy to pastor—they're not perfect, but they want to grow and be developed. Other people are more difficult. They won't take coaching. They always have an excuse. This is hard for me because I want to help everyone.

What I've found is that God always supernaturally makes up for my weaknesses and helps people who want to be coached get to their destiny.

He'll do the same for you.

Discussion Questions

1. When was the last time you asked for help from a mentor or a coach? What makes this difficult?

2. If we asked the people closest to you whether or not you had a coachable attitude, what do you think they would say?

Leadership Challenge

— Give yourself permission to invest in your development.
— Develop a coachable attitude—thank your coach/mentor the next time they correct you.

3

Rhythm vs. Balance

We live in a world filled with opportunities:

- Start your own business.
- Dominate the marketplace and transform your business into the industry leader.
- Meet the woman of your dreams and develop a smoking-hot romance.
- Turn that romance into the ideal marriage and home life.
- Raise the most impressive children in the history of mankind.
- Coach your children to championship seasons in soccer, football, basketball, and baseball.
- Become an endurance athlete and compete on the weekends.
- Follow your favorite sports franchise, every game, every offseason move, year round.
- Travel to the world's most exotic locations.
- Build your dream home.
- Go back to school and get an advanced degree.

- Collect enough big-game trophies to fill your man cave.
- Spend your weekends at a lake house with the fastest boat and coolest jet skis.

Oh, and by the way, do all of this without being stressed out while also maintaining healthy relationships with every person you meet.

Let me know how it goes.

One of the solutions that experts have attempted to offer this conundrum is often referred to as "work-life balance." This sounds inspiring and genuinely helpful. Balance is a peaceful word. Mr. Miyagi told Daniel-san that balance was the key to life.

The problem is, nothing in life stays balanced. Balance is a mythical goal you temporarily find as you keep stacking additional Jenga pieces until the whole thing comes crashing down.

Not a big deal when you're playing a family board game. But when it's your life falling apart, the consequences are much more costly.

Work-life balance is a unicorn. It doesn't exist. The entire premise is flawed. It suggests, *Keep stacking as much as you possibly can until you come right to the edge where everything will fall. Now live the rest of your life in this condition.*

Sounds peaceful.

I like how Tim Ferriss describes this inconsistency: "When people strive for work/life balance, they end up blending them. That's how you end up checking email all day Saturday."[4]

The Bible offers us a far superior alternative: rhythm, not balance. God is into rhythm and seasons, not work-life balance.

You can't find a single passage in the Bible recommending balance as a meaningful life strategy, but you can find many about cooperating with the rhythm of the season God's placed you in.

"There is a time for everything, and a season for every activity under the heavens" (Ecclesiastes 3:1).

You don't wear shorts when it's snowing. Accountants don't plan a vacation in the beginning of April. You don't go back to school for a master's degree when you've just started a business. The problem is not wearing shorts, going on vacation, or getting a master's degree—each of these are great things. The problem is timing.

As the Bible says, "There is a time for everything." Living in rhythm with God means you understand making the right choice at the right time.

Three Ways We Can Live in Rhythm with God

1. We recognize and enjoy the season we're in.
We've never been more aware of what we don't have. It's a powerful motivator. Sociologists have given this phenomenon a name. They call it "FOMO," the fear of missing out.

When we feel like we're missing out, we feel the pull of trying to stack as many things on our plate as possible. We've been told for so long that we can have it all, we've started to believe it. This challenge is exacerbated by our social media culture constantly reminding us of all the things our friends and acquaintances are doing.

We all fall into this trap if we're not intentional. Everything in our culture moves in this direction. God offers a different approach— recognize your season and celebrate it. Enjoy it.

Each season of life offers strengths and weaknesses.

Being single offers you tremendous freedom but can often be lonely. Dating, engaged, or newly married couples typically enjoy powerful emotions and spontaneous schedules but may not have deep roots. Parents of young children struggle to articulate how much they love their new additions but are always tired and can't remember what date night felt like.

You get the idea.

Making the choice to recognize the distinct responsibilities and privileges of your season helps you to say no. This may sound limiting, but it's actually helpful.

Parenting during the teen years is tiring and demanding, but before we know it, we look up and we're an empty nester feeling alone, wondering what life is supposed to look like. This transition goes from painful to enjoyable when we recognize and enjoy the season we're in.

Because, whether we like it or not, a new season is coming.

2. We're honest about our capacity.

When you're young, you think you can do everything. I know I did. But as you get a little older, you realize you have clear strengths and weaknesses. And you learn to acknowledge your limitations.

YOU CAN'T SAY YES TO EVERYTHING.

It makes us feel strong to take on any challenge, but it doesn't change what we can effectively handle.

When we ignore the rhythm and seasons of life and try to do too much, not only do we experience more stress, but we also become less productive.

The real challenge is when we ignore our limits and push our stress threshold—and then we experience a crisis. Because we're already overcommitted, there's no margin left to draw from. This is how marriages get fractured, partnerships get ruined, jobs are lost, credit is destroyed, and bodies shut down.

Obviously, I'm a proponent of growth and increasing our capacity, but not at the expense of reality. When we're honest about the season and our limits, we're free to work really hard and produce results. And the best part is, because we've been intentional, this productivity takes place in the areas we care about most.

Again, a seasonal, God-rhythm mentality helps us live this way. It empowers us to understand the difference between "no" and "not now." Those two responses are not the same. Saying "no" to a goal or a dream is not saying "never."

"Not now" gives us something to look forward to and allows us to pursue the right goal in the right season.

3. We manage our energy more than our time.
When I first started studying leadership, the primary solution to productivity was increased efficiency through time management. There's certainly some value to this approach.

However, over the past few years, my emphasis has shifted. I'm sure you can relate to coming to a meeting or a conversation you had time for, but you couldn't find the energy or motivation to engage. You wished you were anywhere else in the world.

Some guys are morning people and feel productive at 4:30 a.m. Other guys prefer a later start and can easily work well into the night. Whatever our rhythms, we all have a set amount of energy—and once it's gone, it's gone.

I feel more productive and enjoy life more when I match my high-energy moments with my high-energy tasks. I don't try to run at maximum output all day long. Instead, I find ways to anticipate the needs of the day and plan accordingly so I have the appropriate levels of energy for the work I'm going to accomplish.

This is especially important for dads. If you give all of your best energy at work and come home to retreat away from the emotional needs of your family, whether you intend it or not, you're communicating that your work is more important than your loved ones.

But if you prioritize those moments at home, reserve some energy, and recharge before you engage with them, they'll feel valued and important.

What I've found to be helpful in this process is building a general budget—the same way I would with finances. I look at my calendar and portion out daily, weekly, monthly, quarterly, and yearly energy demands. I take into account the rhythm of the family's calendar as well as regular time with my wife to continue to invest in our relationship.

A budget can't account for everything—especially a major challenge or crisis—but I've found having a clear plan makes it far less stressful to account for disruptions. In fact, financial planners tell us one of the primary benefits of a budget is to give you the ability to say no. If it's not in the budget, you don't do it. This works the same way with our calendar.

Discussion Questions

1. What's the biggest difference between balance and rhythm?

2. How would your life look different if you managed your energy more than your time?

Leadership Challenge

— Find one specific goal/dream to put in your "not now" category.
— Save some energy today when you go home so you can engage with each person in your family.
— Build a first draft of your personal energy budget.

The Value of Rest

You can't live in rhythm with God if you don't learn how to rest.

I realize this sounds basic—who needs to learn how to rest? However, if we're honest, we all could learn to do better in this area of our lives.

Forty percent of Americans get less than six hours of sleep per night. By contrast, in 1910, the average American slept nine hours per night. This makes sense because they didn't have smartphones, email, the internet, or Netflix. They weren't trying to binge-watch a season of TV in three nights.

In 2014, the CDC declared sleep deprivation a public health epidemic. Not only does drowsiness lead to an increase in automobile accidents and deaths, but it's also been proven to dramatically increase the risk of serious disease.[5]

While the biblical concept of rest includes peaceful sleep, there's more to it.

Rest is not escaping your responsibilities.
Rest is not shutting yourself away from the outside world.
Rest is not quitting, giving up, or a sign of weakness.

And rest is not a vacation—anyone who has ever taken their family on an expensive, bucket-list level trip knows the demoralizing sensation of returning to work feeling completely exhausted.

Every dad has thought, *I need a vacation—from this vacation*. Veteran dads keep this little nugget to themselves; the rookies tell their wives, which creates a whole new set of challenges. Or so I've been told.

Work is not the problem. Work is good. God created us to work.

The Bible says there's profit in all hard work—no matter what kind of work you're doing.[6] Many of us, especially our younger generations, have lost sight of this.

Contrary to popular opinion, work existed before sin entered the world. You can make a strong case that there will be work in heaven, because when we use our gifts to serve others, we experience fulfillment in our souls.

This is why a transition to a version of retirement that doesn't include using your talents to benefit others is dissatisfying. It's also one of the reasons why lottery winners are no less depressed than the general public.

So, what is biblical rest? In the first few paragraphs of the Bible, we see God rest from His work. He wasn't tired. He wasn't stressed. He doesn't sleep. He didn't need anything.

Instead, He was modeling something for us. The rhythm of a week includes both hard work and intentional rest. He wants us to recognize this pattern of setting aside a part to remind ourselves that everything comes from Him. This is true whether you're talking about your time, your talents, or your money.

The biblical word for this day of rest is the *Sabbath*. When God gave Moses the Ten Commandments, this was the fourth instruction and the only time God said, "Remember."[7]

I don't think God was spicing up His list with a little variety—He used this word on purpose because He knew we'd be tempted to either forget it or flat out ignore it. There's always another project to get to. There's always another report to go over, an email to return, or an escape luring our attention.

We think if we work harder and push further, we'll accomplish more.

GOD WANTS US TO REMEMBER THAT HE'S OUR SOURCE.

Well-intended people have gone to great lengths to enforce this concept as an incredibly strict rule, to the point where it gets silly. Jesus messed with these kinds of people because they missed the whole purpose of what it's for.

He's not keeping score when we deviate from a formula.
He's not mad at us for being stressed.
He's not surprised we get weighed down and anxious with the pressures of life.
He made it so simple.

"Come to me, all you who are weary and burdened, and I will give you rest." – Jesus
(Matthew 11:28)

I get it. At this point, you're thinking, *Okay, Jeff, when I'm stressed at work, and everything at home is hectic, and everyone wants something, and the pressure is intense, I'm supposed to "come to Jesus."*

I'm self-aware enough to realize this sounds super-spiritual and impractical. I don't blame you for thinking this seems unrealistic. But I believe it's possible.

I don't believe rest is the result of everything going exactly how you want it to. I know this because I've had days when I've done only the things I wanted and I didn't feel any more refreshed.

And yet, there have been days when my circumstances or problems did not magically go away, but I ended the day feeling an indescribable peace and a renewed confidence that everything was going to be okay.

What's the biggest difference between these two scenarios? It's really simple. Biblical rest comes from acknowledging and trusting in your true source. Not only does this kind of rest renew your energy and strength, but it also fills you with a motivation to get back to the work God created you to do.

In order to benefit from it, you have to prioritize it. You have to guide your mind, your will, and your emotions into a place of trust and reliance on God. We call this your soul—it's the deepest part of who you are. It longs to be connected to God.

"RETURN TO YOUR REST, MY SOUL, FOR THE LORD HAS BEEN GOOD TO YOU" (PSALM 116:7).

So how does this work? How do you know if you're experiencing this?

How Do We Receive the Rest God Has for Us?

1. Create clear boundaries for your attention/priorities.

Too many of us live in a constant state of partial attention. We're at work but we're distracted by what's happening at home or with our kids at school. We're at home talking with our spouse but we're looking at the latest email from the office on our phone. We're never fully present in the place we're in.

And then we wonder why we can't slow down our minds long enough to rest.

Strong boundaries help this confusion. If your bed is the place you sleep, your body will take it as a signal when your head hits the pillow. But if you consistently work in bed or use technology, you lose the muscle memory that leads to quick, deep sleep.

In the same way, if you confine your work to one room in the house, you'll have a better chance of keeping it from spilling over into playing with the kids or spending time with your spouse.

With very few exceptions, multi-tasking means doing multiple things at a sub-standard level. Clear, focused attention within intentional boundaries is the more productive option.

Technology makes this very difficult because it allows you to work or communicate wherever you are. If you have teenagers or young adults, you understand how easily devices can hijack family time and attention. We're all vulnerable to this trap.

If it's possible, set aside one day out of the week for no screens or devices. Believe it or not, life will continue on without you and you'll experience a greater level of energy once you turn it back on.

2. Establish a daily/weekly/monthly/quarterly routine.

Work is not the enemy of rest. Neither is stress. In fact, both work and stress, when managed properly, allow you to appreciate a greater level of rest. Vacation is not a waste of time. Vacation all the time is a waste of your life.

There's no such thing as instantaneous burnout. If you find yourself constantly daydreaming about a break, you'll do what it takes to get one. Each night, take a look at the rhythm and pace of the next day, and set up key windows to rest—even if it's only for a few minutes. This level of intentionality will create greater self-awareness and productivity.

Once you get a handle on a day, apply this same strategy to your week, your month, and even your quarter. This may sound unrealistic and overly administrative, but your ability to establish a clear rhythm will increase dramatically.

You'll get more done with less stress.

You'll realize what Christ-followers have discovered for centuries: You're more productive working six days and resting one than you are grinding on all seven.

This is the power of the Sabbath. It's a weekly reminder that your source is God—not your ability to push harder. You will enjoy your life more when you set aside a day to worship with your family, turn off your phone, maybe even take a nap, and generally slow down. Even with the weight of humanity on His shoulders, Jesus took naps.

3. Recognize the impact of identity on your ability to rest.
When we don't feel like we're winning at work, we lose sight of what's going on at home. When we're struggling with our spouse, we can't focus on our other responsibilities. When things are difficult with one of the kids, we try to buy their affection or give them whatever they want.

We'll do whatever it takes to get back to a good place—because we can't rest until we get there. The problem is, this makes us desperate, heightens the influence of our emotions, and causes us to make poor choices.

There is no rest when you're afraid you're disappointing the people you care about the most.

The only way out of this trap is to find your identity in the One who created you—the One who loved you and called you good before you did anything to earn or desire this approval. You'll find rest for your soul in His approval.

When you try to be the center of your life, when you try to keep the world spinning, you'll find yourself frustrated and worn down. You can't control the people you love. You can't control every circumstance in your work. When you try, it only wears you out and leaves you frustrated.

GOD DOESN'T ASK YOU TO DO HIS PART—HE'S GOT IT UNDER CONTROL. ONCE YOU ACCEPT THIS, YOU CAN REST.

This is the best understanding of the Sabbath—resting in the goodness of God and His loving approval. Hebrews 4:9-10 tells us this rest is still available for those willing to receive it: "There remains, then, a Sabbath-rest for the people of God; for anyone who enters God's rest also rests from their works, just as God did from his."

Discussion Questions

1. How would you describe the quality of your sleep? When was the last time you felt truly rested?

2. What are you going to do practically to regularly experience biblical rest?

Leadership Challenge

— Simply pray, and ask God to take your worries in exchange for His rest.
— Identify and enforce the boundaries between your work and home.
— On your day off, see if you can take an 8-hour break from technology.

5

How Do We Live a Significant Life/Leave a Legacy?

Men keep score. We can't help it. We want to know where we stand. Leaders set goals and evaluate results. We value data and metrics more today than ever before.

This can be incredibly helpful—but only when we know our highest objectives. In order to know if we're winning, we have to determine which scoreboards we care about most.

Because every one of us has multiple scoreboards: net worth, personal health, relationship with our spouse, relationship with our children, career fulfillment, etc. This isn't an exhaustive list, but it does demonstrate the challenge of trying to manage what it means to win or be successful.

All of these coexist and fluctuate throughout the course of our lives. At any given time, we may be winning in some while losing in others.

Young men want it all. Our future feels limitless. We want to dominate on every scoreboard and our surplus of energy and passion allows us to overlook the inherent conflict between multiple intended outcomes.

As we get older, we begin to see the problem with this approach. When we say yes to one thing, we're also saying no to many others. In order to make these choices, we have to decide what we care about most.

Successful people learn to love the grind. That's what separates people who consistently win from those who make excuses. The problem is that we can become addicted to this cycle of grinding and winning at the expense of the big picture.

I grew up hunting and fishing. And I'm not just trying to catch or kill—I'm coming back with something bigger than you.

I never thought I'd be a runner, but my wife asked me to start doing distance runs with her for fun. I realize I'm never going to win, but I can't shut off the part of my brain pushing me to beat the people around me.

Jesus recognizes this pattern in us better than we do. He sees the potential challenges and heartache this process can leave us with if we're not careful. The only thing worse than losing is winning in an area that doesn't matter. A trophy from a contest you don't care about becomes trash.

"WHAT GOOD IS IT FOR SOMEONE TO GAIN THE WHOLE WORLD, YET FORFEIT THEIR SOUL?" – JESUS (MARK 8:36)

We want to win. We want to collect trophies. We want to gain the whole world. *Who wouldn't?* The question is, what are we willing to give up in order to get it? Would you trade your health? Would you give up your family? How about your soul?

Very few people would say yes, but millions end up there unintentionally because they never take the time to honestly look at their lives and examine their priorities.

Clarity requires priority. When we ignore the difficult process of determining what we care about most, we're always left with unmet expectations.

Perhaps the best way to do this is to begin with the end in mind.

As a pastor, I'm not unfamiliar with the end. I've been with many families as the patriarch is on his deathbed. These moments have indelibly marked me. There's no time for course correction. There's no time to adjust two-, five-, or ten-year plans.

In those moments, you come face to face with your legacy. You're left with the results of the scoreboard you prioritized most. Your legacy is your identity in reverse. What you invested in, what you sowed, what you cared about most—this is what you will leave behind.

Most of us don't naturally start here and work backward. Typically, the continuum moves from success to significance before eventually turning toward legacy.

I understand this now at a deeper level. On October 29, 2019, my hero left this world surrounded by his children and his grandchildren, who thanked him and promised to carry on his legacy. My dad stepped into eternity, and I had the privilege of honoring him by preaching for him one last time. He told people I was his favorite preacher.

The celebration service ended with a video we shot before he passed. He preached at his own funeral. You don't see that often. His words carried so much meaning: "Somebody else will live in your house. Somebody else will drive your car. Somebody else will spend your money. The only thing you leave behind is your reputation and your family."

When we're young, most of us are consumed with being successful. We want to prove we've got what it takes. We want the approval of our peers, our dads, our mentors, and most of all, our own sense of self. As long as these remain out of reach, you'll continue to chase success.

The problem is, this concept is often fluid and elusive. Because of this, it's possible to get stuck on an endless treadmill chasing an abstract notion of success until the very end.

If we're able to gain a sense of accomplishment and success, then our attention shifts to significance.

We need to know we matter, our efforts are not in vain, and our triumphs will be remembered. We think, *How would my company, my peer group, and the people who I respect respond to my absence?* This can be a painful exercise, but I've found that once a man checks this box off in his mind, his attention moves to the issue of legacy.

LEGACY ONLY BEGINS ONCE YOU'RE GONE.

Legacy answers the question, "What was the lasting impact of your life?"

Alexander the Great became the king of the Macedonian Empire at age twenty. He never lost a battle, he conquered the known world, and he had twenty cities named in his honor. This is an astonishing list of accomplishments. His impact was never greater than at the height of his reign.

By contrast, Jesus never commanded an earthly army, never sat on an earthly throne, and spent thirty years in obscurity before teaching and ministering to crowds of people for three years. Upon His death, His ragtag group of followers grew from twelve to thousands to more than two billion around the world today.

That's legacy.

We're not trying to equal Alexander or Jesus, but one strategy clearly has a longer impact than the other.

How Do We Leave a Legacy?

1. Decide which scoreboard matters the most.

Begin with the end in mind. We don't get to choose how we die, but we do get to choose what we value while we're alive.

- Is your relationship with God more important than your accomplishments?

- Is your relationship with your spouse more important than your hobbies?

- Is your relationship with your children more important than your next promotion?

- Does the prioritization of your energy, time, and resources reflect these values?

I'm not anti-hobbies, promotions, or accomplishments—I believe they each have value. But we have to make sure they're in the right order if we want to win in the areas we care about the most.

Every man has to decide what he's going to prioritize—no one else can do it for you. I've worked with people long enough to realize that in the end we do what we want.

However, if we're followers of Christ, there has to be an eternal component to what we're investing in. If we direct our time, talent, and treasure to things without eternal significance, sooner or later they'll fade away.

2. Develop a basic life plan.

Once you decide which scoreboards matter the most, begin to think about what you want your life to look like when you come to the end.

- What kind of person do you want to become?
- What do you want the theme of your life to be?

- What do you want your relationship with your spouse to look like?
- What do you want your relationship with your children and your grandchildren to look like?
- What kinds of friendships and mentoring relationships would you like to have?

Describe these with a level of detail and then ask yourself, "What am I doing today in order to take steps toward that goal?" In this respect, relationships are similar to any other investment: what you put in them today determines what they look like down the road.

3. Give from your heart to something bigger than you that will outlast you.

After you've decided what matters the most and you've drafted a basic outline to help you get there, ask yourself what it will cost you to make this a reality. It won't happen on its own. It will require you to sacrificially set aside time, money, and energy to make these goals a reality.

Jesus said that there's an undeniable connection between our treasure and our heart. Where one goes, the other follows. If you show me your bank ledger, I'll show you what you care about. People who leave a legacy prioritize their giving to the things they value most.

I have a clear picture of where I'm headed.

When I'm coming to the end, I'm not going to take another look at my trophies or accomplishments. I won't be focused on the numbers in my accounts. I want to be surrounded by my family—both my natural and spiritual family, the people I've loved and served. I want them to say, "Thank you so much for investing in us. We'll take it from here."

This picture burns so bright on the inside of me, it changes the way I live. I'm constantly asking myself, "Am I prioritizing and investing what it's going to take to make this a reality?"

Discussion Questions

1. How do you define success? Do you feel like you've achieved it?

2. At this point in your life, are you more driven to be significant or to leave a legacy?

3. If you were to keep your priorities the same, what would your legacy be? Would you be satisfied with your lasting impact?

Leadership Challenge

— Evaluate your scoreboards based on what you're actually doing, not on what you'd like to do.
— Be honest about the gaps between where you are and where you're trying to go.
— Be prepared to share your basic life plan outline with the group.

The Winning Fundamentals

Spiritual Foundations

6

How Can I Have a Relationship with God?

Sin & Salvation

So God created mankind in his own image, in the image of God he created them; male and female he created them. God blessed them and said to them, "Be fruitful and increase in number; fill the earth and subdue it."
Genesis 1:27-28a

For we are God's handiwork, created in Christ Jesus to do good works, which God prepared in advance for us to do.
Ephesians 2:10

You are not an accident. You are more than a collection of atoms. Your life is significant and filled with deep meaning. There is a purpose for your life.

You were made to be with God. Think about that.

THE INFINITE, ETERNAL, UNCREATED GOD NOT ONLY KNOWS YOUR NAME, EVERY DETAIL OF YOUR LIFE, AND ALL YOUR DEEPEST FEARS AND HOPES, BUT HE ALSO WANTS TO HAVE A RELATIONSHIP WITH YOU.

This message is clear throughout all of Scripture. We were created in the image of God—to look like Him and to add our part in reflecting His goodness to the rest of the world.

This word "handiwork" from Ephesians 2 is meant to evoke the product of a master craftsman who skillfully and intentionally develops each piece. Another version chooses the word "masterpiece." And you're not meant to sit on a shelf or hang in a museum.

You have gifts and abilities entrusted to you to be shared for the benefit of others.

When life works the way God designed it, you use your gifts to bless and serve others with pure motivation because you know you're loved and approved by God. This allows you to benefit others without an expectation in return. For your service, you experience fulfillment and joy, and God receives glory. It's this incredible, life-giving cycle that adds value to everyone.

Now I realize this may sound naïve and ideal, but it's what the Bible says. You were created in God's image to enjoy with Him everything He made, as you use your gifts to steward all you've been given.

If you've ever wondered why you wanted to travel the world and experience all life has to offer, now you know why. It's why people often say they feel closer to God in the mountains or overlooking a breathtaking view.

If you've ever wanted to use your gifts in meaningful work for something bigger than yourself, this is the reason. It's why people often say they're inspired watching an artist or a craftsman use their talents. We were created to live this way.

While we sometimes experience momentary glimpses of this reality, these moments are rare and fleeting. Regular, everyday life has all kinds of problems. We can't get it how we want it, and even when we do, it doesn't deliver like we expect. And most of the time, we're not sure how God fits into what we're doing. We feel separate and distant from Him.

What keeps us from enjoying the life we were created to live in a genuine relationship with a perfect God? To find the answer, let's go to the Bible and read the nine verses that lead up to the promise of Ephesians 2:10.

READ Ephesians 2:1-9 and answer the following questions from the passage:

1. Because of transgressions and sins, everyone is born spiritually _____.

2. How many of us lived this way?

3. Do we become this way when we make bad choices, or is it in our nature?

4. How does someone who is spiritually dead become alive?

---

5. What phrase does verse 8 use to describe this process?

*Section 2 Answer Key located on pp. 365-366

The reason you can't live the life you were created to live is because you can't live a perfect life with a perfect God if you're not perfect.

Even the best among us realize we're not perfect. We make mistakes. We hurt others with our words and choices—often the people we love the most. And the problem in this passage goes deeper than what we do or say—it even extends to what we want and what we think.

You see, the thing about a perfect God is, He knows us so completely that He sees past our poker face to what's really going on inside us. If you're a dad, you've experienced a small piece of this when your kid is pouting. You ask them what's wrong and they refuse to tell you.

We don't need help feeling guilty. We feel guilty because we *are* guilty. We know we come up short. The world is a broken place; real evil exists out there. But the deeper problem isn't the evil that's "out there"—it's the capacity for evil on the inside of us that's truly terrifying.

This tendency, which can be found in exactly every human being who has ever lived, is called sin. Not only do we make mistakes we come to regret, but we often know what the right choice is and instead choose the thing we know is wrong because it's what we want.

Most of us give ourselves too much credit. This is fundamental to the human condition. Psychologists call this self-serving bias. We all have the tendency to take credit for any success around us while we blame others for our mistakes. As a culture, we cling to the idea that we're all basically good, but we wouldn't like the results if someone followed us and kept score of every sinful deed, thought, and desire we had—even for one day.

So, what can we do with the problem of sin?

One option is to try really hard to be perfect.

It doesn't work. It's exhausting. And it's the fastest way to become aware of how messed up everyone else is because they're not trying as hard as you are to do the right thing. Trying to be perfect is a guaranteed approach to make your life miserable.

A second option is to decide that because we're not perfect, God's not perfect either.

The problem with this option is that we end up with a god who looks like us. This gives a great boost to our pride but the value wears off really quickly. A god like us doesn't have much to offer.

The third option is to find someone who is perfect to be a substitute on our behalf.

I was thinking about this one day at the airport while I was waiting in a really long security line. Like everyone else, I was frustrated. We were waiting for our turn to be examined in order to gain admittance to the other side by stepping into the big gray machine that spins and takes your picture.

The security people were telling everyone to take out their laptops, take off their shoes—you know the song-and-dance routine. If you travel semi-regularly and pay even moderate attention, you understand there are some things they'll never let through.

Imagine if one of those nonnegotiable items wasn't packed in your carry-on—it was in your heart. You can't take it off like shoes, a belt, or a watch. You can't throw it out like a knife or a bottle containing more than 3.5 fluid ounces.

It's part of you.

In that situation, the only chance you have to get to the other side is if someone else gets in the scanner for you. And when the security team looks at the scan, they don't see you.

This is precisely what Ephesians 2 is describing. This is what Jesus did on the cross.

Because God is perfect, He can't allow evil and injustice to continue without being dealt with. This leaves two options: (1) eternal separation from God, or (2) the evil and dead are made righteous and alive to be with God forever.

In 2 Corinthians 5:21, Paul says it this way: "God made him who had no sin to be sin for us, so that in him we might become the righteousness of God."

The word "righteousness" is a legal word meaning "right-standing." It's a condition conferred upon the innocent or the perfect. Because we couldn't live the perfect life we were created for, Jesus came and lived it in our place.

JESUS EXCHANGED HIS PERFECTION FOR OUR GUILT.

We didn't deserve it and we couldn't earn it. Jesus lived the life we should have lived but couldn't. He died the death we deserved in our place. This is why Ephesians says we have been saved from what we deserved by faith—putting our trust in what Jesus did for us, not in our ability to save ourselves.

And this is why this miracle is called a gift of God. The Greek word for grace is *charis* and it simply means "gift." There's nothing for us to brag or boast about.

The fancy theological word for this is "justification." When we put our trust (faith) in what Jesus did for us, God doesn't look at our righteousness or our perfect obedience, but at His perfect moral record. As a result, we receive the love and approval God has for Jesus for all eternity.

This is why we don't clean ourselves up to enter into a relationship with Jesus. We'll never be clean enough. The real starting place is recognizing our utter inability to produce a relationship with God any other way.

Being nice to people, following spiritual rules, giving to the poor, knowing lots of facts about the Bible—these things have value and may improve the quality of our lives, but they don't have the power to save us.

Only trusting in the perfect obedience and love of Jesus can do that. Because of this, we receive access to God's original plan—to live the life we were created to live.

I realize this may not be easy.

Many of us have to overcome barriers in our minds. We feel like this applies to someone else but not us. For example, the pain of poor choices can lead you to believe you're beyond hope. Or you feel like because of what someone else did to you, you'll never be able to completely put those painful experiences behind you.

Jesus spoke to people in both of these groups—and He helped them overcome these challenges.

Next, it's not easy to be honest and humble enough to admit your need for a Savior when you're self-sufficient and accustomed to success. It's difficult, especially for a grown man, to admit he comes up short. But on the other side of this willingness, you'll discover a power far beyond your own ability.

Finally, there's often a hesitation from this simple thought: *Can I live up to this?* It sounds so compelling, so exciting, which only increases the pressure. No one wants to fail. No one wants to be a hypocrite. But when you understand that your ability to live this way is not a function of your willpower, you're free to step into this new life in Christ.

Discussion Questions

1. How does this description of what it means to have a relationship with God differ from what you previously thought?

2. Do you have any hesitation or reluctance to take this new step because of how you were raised? Are you worried about how you would explain this to your family?

3. Do you have this kind of a relationship with God? Would you like to? What's holding you back?

7

How Do I Change and Begin My New Life in Christ?

Repentance & Baptism

Godly sorrow brings repentance that leads to salvation and leaves no regret, but worldly sorrow brings death.
2 Corinthians 7:10

I preached that they should repent and turn to God and demonstrate their repentance by their deeds.
Acts 26:20b

Change is a constant in life, but it's not easy. We spend a lot of time and energy trying to figure it out. You're reading this book because you want to grow and change.

It can be fun to think about change. It's more difficult to actually do it.

We like the benefits of change more than we like the process. All change begins with the painful realization of where you really are—not where you'd like to be, not your idealized sense of self, not a slightly lesser version of someone you admire.

You have to see the real you. You have to confront the brutal facts. As painful as this can be, it's a gift because it reveals your need to change.

Once you get the brutal facts, you have two options: (1) receive it and change, or (2) resist and stay trapped.

- If you want to lose weight, you don't get mad at the scale or call it a liar.
- If you want to grow in professional skills, you don't argue with your coaching assessment.
- If you want to be a better friend, you don't attack them when they give you honest feedback.

This is what 2 Corinthians 7 describes as the difference between worldly sorrow and godly sorrow. Worldly sorrow is feeling sorry for yourself because you were challenged or critiqued. You don't feel bad for what you did—you feel bad because you were called on it.

Worldly sorrow has no power to change you. Instead, the self-pity typically drives you right back into the poor choices you made in the first place.

Godly sorrow is a whole different ballgame. You see yourself from a right perspective and you're willing to do whatever it takes to change. People who are willing to learn, even when it's painful, end up changing and growing. The Bible calls this "repentance."

It's important to understand that repentance is a gift from God. It's not you beating yourself up to prove you're sorry. Romans 2:4 reminds us not to overlook God's kindness, tolerance, and patience because it's this kindness from God that leads us to repentance.

"Repentance" feels like a church word. It sounds spiritual and heavy, and it's not always clear. The word simply means "to change your mind." It was a military term used to describe a marching soldier who did an about-face—stopping, turning, and proceeding in the opposite direction.

- It's more than telling God you're sorry.
- It's more than a promise to stop your bad habits.
- It's more than a prayer you pray so you can enter heaven when you die.

REPENTANCE IS A TURNING *FROM* YOUR OLD WAY OF THINKING: *FROM* YOUR SINFUL NATURE, *FROM* SATISFYING YOUR SELFISH DESIRES.

BUT IT'S ALSO A TURNING *TO*: *TO* A NEW LIFE IN CHRIST, *TO* A NEW WAY TO SEE YOURSELF AND OTHERS, AND *TO* A LIFE PRODUCING FRUIT THAT HONORS GOD.

Acts 26 makes it clear that true repentance is more than a private, internal change of heart. When repentance is genuine, when it comes from godly sorrow, what begins with a change in mind naturally produces a change in deeds. You don't just think differently; you act differently.

This has been the pattern from the very first followers of Jesus. In Acts 2, Peter preaches the first sermon after Jesus ascends to heaven and fills them with His power. There is a massive crowd of people gathered—we don't know how many were there, but we know about 3,000 people responded to Peter's message.

READ Acts 2:36-39 and answer the following questions from the passage:

1. What did Peter mean when he tells the people that they crucified Jesus?

2. What happened to the people when they heard Peter's message? What does that mean?

3. When the people asked, "Brothers, what shall we do. . ." what did Peter tell them?

4. Who is this promise for?

Throughout the book of Acts and the rest of the New Testament, there is a clear connection between repentance and baptism. When a person puts their trust in Christ, they repent *from* their old way of thinking—their natural thoughts and desires—*to* a new life, putting their hope in Jesus to make them right with God. Baptism is the public expression of this inward change.

Baptism was a historical, religious purification ceremony. Jesus gave it new meaning and significance as an expression of what God had done in us. When He was baptized, God's voice could be heard declaring, "This is My Son in whom I'm well pleased." When we put our trust in Jesus and receive His righteousness by faith, we receive the same approval and affirmation from the Father.

Romans 6:3-4 describes baptism as a picture of sharing in both the death and burial of Jesus as well as His resurrection to a new life. Baptism does not make us right with God—Jesus' death and resurrection on our behalf accomplished this. Baptism is not a celebration of what we do for God; it's a public celebration of the joining of a believer to the power of what Jesus accomplished.

It's far more than a religious ceremony or tradition. It's an intentional, relational step of faith that lets the whole world know we're committed to Jesus and His new life at work in us.

Jesus told His followers to do two things with new disciples in Matthew 28:19-20: baptize them and teach them to obey everything He'd commanded.

Baptism is a one-time step of faith to celebrate genuine repentance to a new life in Christ.

Repentance begins as a one-time decision to turn your life of sin to a new life in Christ, but it is also the bedrock of a new way of living.

It is the daily commitment to change and obey as the Spirit of God leads and guides us. This is called the process of sanctification—the lifelong journey of becoming the person God created us to be as we continue to follow Jesus. Martin Luther famously said that the Christian life is marked by repentance.

The natural, healthy response for a Christian who makes a poor choice is not to give up on his faith, to get re-baptized, or to question whether his relationship with God was ever genuine. It's simply to repent—to turn from the unhealthy thoughts/attitudes/actions that move us away from Jesus and to move toward Him.

Discussion Questions

1. What is the difference between biblical repentance and feeling bad for something we did or didn't do? Where does the gift of repentance come from?

2. What does repentance mean? What do you turn from and turn to?

3. Is water baptism more than a traditional religious ceremony? Why?

8

What Does God Want from Me?

Lordship & Obedience

If you love me, you will keep my commandments. – Jesus
John 14:15 ESV

*Therefore let all Israel be assured of this: God has made
this Jesus, whom you crucified, both Lord and Messiah.*
Acts 2:36 NIV

But set Christ apart as Lord in your hearts.
1 Peter 3:15a NET

Once we put our trust in Jesus, repent from our sin, and publicly declare our faith in Him through baptism, what does God want from us next? The same thing He's always wanted: our hearts.

He doesn't immediately whisk us away to heaven or sequester us off to a monastery to purely focus on spiritual disciplines. So, how does this work? What does it mean to give God our hearts?

Jesus told His disciples in John 14 that the way they showed they loved Him was to obey what He said. This is His "love language." We demonstrate our love for Him by becoming the person He created us to be through obeying what He asked us to do.

People have called Jesus many things—a prophet, a wise teacher, a friend of sinners, the Son of God, Savior—but Acts 2:36 tells us that God made Jesus "Lord." That's who He is whether we recognize it or not.

JESUS CAN'T BE LESS THAN WHO HE IS.

He doesn't say one thing and do another. He has perfect integrity. He's not a hypocrite—He used this term to describe someone who plays a role or acts like someone they're not.

In his subsequent letter after his message in the book of Acts, Peter makes it clear that this is the expected response for all followers of Christ.

Jesus is more than a friend. He's more than a voice in our life. He's more than a ticket to heaven or someone we call when we're in trouble. Peter tells us to set Him apart (the definition of the word "sanctify" preferred by many translations) in our hearts as "Lord."

What does it mean to call someone *Lord*? In a literal sense it means "master." It signifies authority, highest honor, and ultimate allegiance. In the ancient world, it was commonly used in the expression "Caesar is Lord," in recognition of the Roman Emperor as the leader of the world.

Therefore, a first-century person brazen enough to claim that "Jesus is LORD" was making a radical, potentially life-threatening statement. Thousands of the earliest Christ-followers paid the ultimate price for their faith—and this horrific practice still continues in restrictive nations to this day.

We may never face this level of sacrifice, but what does it mean for us to say that Jesus is Lord? How does it change our lives?

READ Luke 6:46-49 and answer the following questions from the passage:

1. What does Jesus expect of people who call Him "Lord"?

2. After we come to Jesus and hear His words, what does He expect us to do?

3. Which man came to Jesus and heard His words: the one with the well-built house or the one that was destroyed?

4. What was the difference between the two?

Jesus is asking why someone would call Him "Lord" if they weren't willing to do what He says.

This may sound heavy. It may sound like it's creating a standard no one could possibly live up to. After all, who could possibly do what Jesus says at all times? We've already discovered that none of us could live up to this in order to earn a relationship with God.

So, what is Jesus after?

Two of the most important words in this passage from Luke 6 are "practice" and "foundation." No one practices with perfect accuracy. Practice is the process of improvement, of changing your patterns based on repetition toward a clearly stated goal. In 1 John 3:10, it says that the children of God are obvious because they practice righteousness.

This doesn't mean they're perfect in their obedience, but it does mean they're making clear progress. This concept is echoed throughout the New Testament.

The other word is "foundation." The foundation is a framework everything else is built on. It determines the shape and function of the rest of what follows. If the foundation of your life is that "Jesus is a wise teacher," or "Jesus is a friend," it will determine how you relate to Him.

IF YOU BUILD ON THE FOUNDATION THAT "JESUS IS LORD," IT MEANS THAT WHEN YOU DON'T AGREE OR UNDERSTAND, YOU COMMIT TO FOLLOW AND OBEY.

It doesn't mean you'll always do everything perfectly, but it does mean you've chosen to give Him final say.

"Lordship" scares us because it feels positional and impersonal. But when the Bible uses this concept, it's far more relational than we imagine.

Five of the prophetic books of the Old Testament use the theme of God as a loving husband to His people. Ezekiel, Jeremiah, Isaiah, Hosea, and

Joel all pick up on this theme in close to 20 different passages. Jesus is well aware of this metaphor, and He picks up on it in all four Gospels. Both 2 Corinthians and Revelation use it. But no other section uses it as clearly as Ephesians 5.

God compares His relationship with His people to a husband and a wife. I realize this is uncommon and hard for us to relate to. Maybe this will help: When a man and a woman exchange vows, they verbally commit to a covenant agreement saying, "I choose you above all others." This is the foundation of their relationship.

On November 18, 1995, I committed my life to my wife, Brandy. She knew I wasn't going to be perfect, but she also trusted that my exclusive commitment to her meant that I willingly gave up my other options.

A marriage relationship is not contingent upon each person's ability to perfectly fulfill the other's expectations. They're making a promise to put each other first for the rest of their lives. They're intentionally restricting their options out of the commitment of their hearts. The implied goal is to grow in love, consideration, and faithfulness for the rest of their lives.

It's not a partial commitment. It's not "You can have my Friday to Sunday, but I can do whatever I want from Monday to Thursday." You bring all of who you are and offer it willingly. We all grow in our ability to live this out, but if we have a genuine relationship with Him, we freely give up our right to say, "You can't have this area of my life."

Now the metaphor breaks down because in our relationships neither party is perfect. But in our relationship with God, He perfectly fulfills and upholds His love for us. He doesn't expect us to reciprocate in our performance—but He does expect perfect faithfulness in our hearts.

The concepts of lordship and obedience cause us to hedge because we don't know if we can live up to it. Obedience motivated by obligation or guilt is weak. Obedience driven by a desire to live up to a perfect spiritual standard fades quickly.

If we have an obedience problem, we really have a love problem. We've lost our way. We've given our hearts to something else.

But in any of our most treasured relationships, the only lasting motivation is love. The same is true in our relationship with God. When we commit to putting Him first, when we offer our whole lives to Him out of love, we grow in our ability to obey and put His words into practice like nothing else.

Discussion Questions

1. In your relationship with Jesus, do you relate to Him as Savior? Do you know Him as your friend? What about Lord?

2. What is the only lasting motivation for obedience? How does this change our approach?

3. Is there any area of your life that's off limits to Jesus? Is there an area where you can sense He wants to become Lord?

9

How Do I Hear from God?

God's Word & Spiritual Hunger

All Scripture is God-breathed and is useful for teaching, rebuking, correcting and training in righteousness.
2 Timothy 3:16

For the word of God is alive and active. Sharper than any double-edged sword, it penetrates even to dividing soul and spirit, joints and marrow; it judges the thoughts and attitudes of the heart.
Hebrews 4:12

Most people respect the Bible. Even if they don't agree with what the Scriptures say, they acknowledge the impact and influence of these 66 ancient books.

However, these same people also struggle to experience that living and active Word in their own lives. Despite our best intentions, Bible literacy has been steadily declining over the past few decades. There are several reasons for this.

The Bible is intimidating. Where do I start? What does it mean? How does it fit together? How does it apply to my life? These are only a few of the most common challenges people encounter when they try to read it.

It's hard to understand, so you have to ask for help. This is often embarrassing, which also makes you want to set it aside and come back later.

Another major problem is finding the time and attention to fully engage. Attention spans are shorter, multi-tasking has become the norm, and digital devices aren't conducive to the kind of prolonged, disciplined reading the Bible requires.

We're faced with a major dilemma: God says that all of His Word is alive and active; it's God-breathed and useful; it has the ability to judge the thoughts and attitudes of our hearts—but we don't know how to get those results.

I've found that the two biggest keys to getting over the obstacles preventing us from learning to hear God through His Word are consistency and authority. It's not a magic bullet, a life hack, or a cheat code. It starts with an old-fashioned disciplined commitment.

First, I'm going to choose to read the Bible every day (even for five minutes). As I begin reading, I'm going to predetermine that when I don't understand or agree with Scripture, I don't change it—it changes me.

Here's the perspective shift that changes everything. The purpose of God's Word is not to study spiritual information, to prepare for an exam to get into heaven, or to memorize Bible trivia.

THE PURPOSE OF THE BIBLE IS TO SHOW US WHO GOD IS. IT'S RELATIONAL.

If God told you, "I'm coming to spend 10 minutes with you to tell you what's on my heart," we'd all make time for Him. But this is precisely what He's done through His Word.

Maybe you've tried this. Maybe you're one of the many who started the "read the Bible in a year" plan and you got stuck on the side of the road in Leviticus. You're not alone. That group has a lot of members.

One of the biggest differences between our lives today and the ancient world is that we're far more individualistic than they were. We think important reading is personal, private, quiet, and solitary. This is not how the people of God read/studied Scripture throughout history. It was done in a group setting, with discussion, with application, with questions, and wrestling.

It was done in the context of families and groups.

In order to grow, you should read the Bible on your own. It's not an either/or situation. We read it alone, but we also benefit when we read it together.

Groups help us see what we can't see. They help us understand how the Bible is one big story—each part helps us understand the rest. It helps us to ask, "What did this mean in its original context?" before we move on to the all-important question, "What does it mean for me now?"

As we grow and learn how to do this together, we strengthen our ability to do it each day on our own—which only increases the quality of the discussions we have when we come back and talk about it together.

This is how we learn anything: study, ask questions, think about it each day, say it out loud, and explain it to someone else.

As we've said from the beginning, when a man gets excited about something—whether it's an investment opportunity, new technology, fantasy football, or any other hobby—he studies up and finds a group of people who can help him grow in his understanding. Learning to hear God through His Word works the same way.

READ Psalm 19:7-14 and answer the following questions from the passage:

1. What are some of the different terms used to describe God's Word?

2. How does verse 7 describe the benefits of God's law? What about His statutes?

3. What do the precepts and commands produce in verse 8?

4. How valuable are they?

5. What advantages does verse 11 promise?

6. When we know God, His laws, and His principles, what does verse 14 describe as the lasting impact?

The purpose of pleasing God with our words and our thoughts is relational.

We want to be close to Him more than we want to memorize information about Him. We want to live in a way that honors Him more than we want to prepare for an exam. When you're close to someone and your relationship is healthy, being with them is a privilege, not a burden or an obligation.

This is such a critical piece for lasting motivation. If we can't connect how reading the Bible brings us into a deeper relationship with God, we'll give up. But once we learn how to find God's voice in His Word, we'll make time to be with Him every day.

JESUS PLACED SUCH INCREDIBLE VALUE ON BEING CLOSE WITH HIS FATHER. HE TOLD THE DISCIPLES ON MULTIPLE OCCASIONS THAT IT WAS MORE VITAL THAN FOOD FOR OUR SURVIVAL.

We've all struggled to understand what God's voice sounds like. Pastors don't have a special hotline to God.

It sounds so basic, but if we want to know what God thinks, if we want to know what He sounds like, if we want to know how to recognize His voice out of the thoughts running through our minds, then we start with His Word.

Joshua 1:8 explains that if we talk about and think about God's Word every day, we will be able to do what it says—which will cause us to be successful. James 1:22 reminds us not to just hear the Word but also to do what it says. Remember how Jesus differentiated the wise and foolish builders in Luke 6? Both heard His words, but only one put them into practice.

It's not about how much of the Bible you know; it's about how much of the Bible you can actually live.

Discussion Questions

1. What is the greatest challenge you face in trying to hear God through His Word on a daily basis (don't understand, don't have time, etc.)?

2. How does the Bible impact the way you speak and the way you think? Give a specific example.

3. Can you think of a specific moral issue where you changed your mind because of what the Bible says? How did it impact your daily life?

10

How Can I Experience God's Presence Every Day?

The Holy Spirit & Spiritual Gifts

If you then, being evil, know how to give good gifts to your children, how much more will your heavenly Father give the Holy Spirit to those who ask Him? – Jesus
Luke 11:13 NASB

But you will receive power when the Holy Spirit comes on you; and you will be my witnesses in Jerusalem, and in all Judea and Samaria, and to the ends of the earth. – Jesus
Acts 1:8 NIV

And you will receive the gift of the Holy Spirit. The promise
is for you and your children and for all who are far off—for
all whom the Lord our God will call.
Acts 2:38b-39 NIV

I know you want to grow closer to God—your choice to read this book is a clear demonstration of this desire. And a significant part of growing closer to God includes a relationship with the Holy Spirit.

You want this, but so many people wrestle with how it works. We can grasp the concept of God. We can relate to Jesus. But I realize that the Holy Spirit often feels like something totally different.

Unfortunately, people often tend to extremes when they talk about the third person of the Trinity. Some never mention Him at all, as if He's been forgotten, while others can't seem to talk about anything without working Him back into the conversation in a way that feels awkward or forced. Because neither approach is healthy, many people end up avoiding the issue altogether.

If we want a relationship with the Holy Spirit, the place we need to start, the standard we need to look to, is the Word of God.

In John 16:7, Jesus told His disciples it was to their advantage (NASB and ESV), it was good (NIV), it was for the best (NLT) that He left them to go to His Father. This is an incredible statement. Peter, James, John, or any of the other disciples would not have believed this in the moment. Why would He make such an outrageous claim?

Because He knew His absence would lead His Father to send them the Holy Spirit. Later in the same passage, Jesus said the Holy Spirit would lead and guide them into all truth.

The three passages at the beginning of the chapter reinforce this radical idea, but they also make it clear we're included in this amazing promise. We can have the same advantage they had.

JESUS SAID THAT OUR HEAVENLY FATHER WILL GIVE THE HOLY SPIRIT TO ANY OF HIS CHILDREN WHO SIMPLY ASK HIM.

Jesus told the disciples the Holy Spirit wouldn't just give them information; the Holy Spirit would give them the power to tell the whole world about Him.

And in his first message, Peter reminds us that the gift of the Holy Spirit is not merely for pastors or some kind of super Christians—it was promised to every single person God called.

According to Jesus and God's Word, there's no reason to feel weird around the Holy Spirit. He's a person, not an "it." He's not a ghost or a dove. He's the third person of the Trinity who has eternally and perfectly loved both Jesus and the Father.

Jesus' most exhaustive teaching on the Holy Spirit (see John 14–17, often called the Farewell Discourse) takes place immediately following the Last Supper on the night before He was crucified. He was preparing His closest friends to experience God's presence in their lives on a daily basis—and in doing so, He prepares all of us who follow Him to do the same.

READ John 14:15-17, 25-27 and answer the following questions from the passage:

1. What is the first thing Jesus calls the Holy Spirit in verse 16?

2. What are the first two things He does?

---

3. How is the Spirit described in verse 17?

4. Does everyone accept the Holy Spirit?

5. According to the end of verse 17, how do we know the Holy Spirit?

6. What does Jesus say the Holy Spirit will do for us in verse 26?

7. Does this impact how we study God's Word? How does the Holy Spirit help us in this area?

Jesus said the Holy Spirit is our helper, our defender, and our counselor. He will be with us forever. He lives both *with* us and *in* us. He teaches us all things and reminds us of what Jesus said. What's weird about that?

In addition to all of these incredible benefits, the Bible outlines three other key contributions from the Holy Spirit.

1. The fruit of the Spirit

In John 15, Jesus told His disciples that apart from Him they could do nothing, but if their relationship with Him stayed strong and healthy, they would bear great fruit. This is a picture of God's plan for us—when we stay connected to Him, He changes the way we live.

Galatians 5:22-23 describes this fruit of the Holy Spirit as love, joy, peace, forbearance, kindness, goodness, faithfulness, gentleness, and self-control. That's a big list! I don't have the emotional energy, the personality, or the temperament to consistently live this way.

But the good news is, these don't grow out of our lives through discipline and willpower; they show up when we live under the influence and guidance of the Holy Spirit. He gives us the power to demonstrate the goodness of God in us and through us.

2. The gifts of the Spirit

Romans 12:5-6 tells us we've been given different gifts through the Spirit, not for our own benefit, but to add value to each other. There are at least three passages of Scripture that include these spiritual gifts— Romans 12:6-8; 1 Corinthians 12:7-11, 27-31; and Ephesians 4:11-12. It's worth your time to go and read them for yourself.

The important principle is to discover your gifts and to use them to serve others—Peter makes this clear in 1 Peter 4:10-11. When this happens, others benefit from your gift, you receive fulfillment, and God receives glory. One of the biggest reasons why people struggle to get connected in the church is that they don't know how to use their gifts to serve others.

I've found that the best remedy to this problem is to jump in and start serving other people. When someone is led by the Holy Spirit on a consistent basis, they're motivated to serve others. Through the process of serving in the context of relationships, their top gifts begin to emerge. As they regularly apply those gifts, both the benefit they add to others and the joy they receive go up.

THE TRAP IS GETTING STUCK THINKING YOU LACK THE RIGHT OPPORTUNITY TO MATCH YOUR GIFTS WITH AN AVAILABLE NEED.

If we'll just start serving and be faithful where we are, the Holy Spirit will help us get to the right spot.

3. The baptism with the Holy Spirit

The Bible makes it clear that when we repent and put our trust in Jesus, we receive His righteousness, His peace with God, and His relationship with the Holy Spirit. But all throughout the New Testament, we see a subsequent interaction with the Holy Spirit. In Acts 1:5, Jesus tells His disciples that John baptized them with water, but later they would be baptized with the Holy Spirit. And then throughout the book of Acts (chapters 8, 10, 11, and 19), we see this process repeated in the lives of followers of Christ.

Remember, justification is a one-time moment we could not earn but we receive by faith. This makes us right with God. In other words, neither water baptism nor baptism with the Holy Spirit saves us. But they do give us a greater ability to experience more of the life God wants us to live. There is tremendous value in our continuing relationship with the Spirit of God.

For example, the disciples put their trust in Jesus, then He breathed His Spirit in them, then He told them to wait in Jerusalem until they received the gift of the Spirit, and then they continued to be filled with the Spirit as they gathered together in prayer and worship. Ephesians 5:18-20 tells us to be filled with the Spirit as we encourage and speak to one another through songs and with grateful hearts to God. The word used in verse 18 may be better understood as an ongoing filling. It's not a one-time event.

Sanctification is the process of grace by which God makes us more and more of who we were created to be. As we learned, water baptism is an act of obedience and a gift in the process of sanctification. In the same way, the baptism with the Holy Spirit is a gift that gives us the help, the power, and the filling Jesus promised to anyone who simply asks.

Discussion Questions

1. Have you ever struggled to relate to the Holy Spirit? If yes, you're definitely not alone. What has made it difficult for you?

2. How was Jesus' description of the Holy Spirit different from what you expected?

11

Where Has God Placed Me?

Spiritual Family

God sets the lonely in families, he leads out the prisoners with singing; but the rebellious live in a sun-scorched land.
Psalm 68:6

But in fact God has placed the parts in the body, every one of them, just as he wanted them to be.
1 Corinthians 12:18

You're on a journey with God. You're developing your spiritual foundations. You have a variety of different options on how to proceed. Here are a few (but not all) of the options available to you:

A. You can make it up as you go along based on what feels right to you.
B. You can hop around to different groups, friends, and churches until you find the perfect place that meets all your needs.
C. You can put it off until later.
D. You can commit to where God has placed you.

Option A is a really popular choice, but in the end it doesn't work because it ultimately sets you up as God.

Option B is more difficult than it seems: *Find a church where you like the preaching, you like the music, the location is convenient, the parking is plentiful, the people are friendly, the coffee is good, the bathrooms are clean with no lines, and there are plenty of programs and opportunities for you to pursue your interests and use your gifts.*

The moment your church fails to provide this, you start looking for a new place that better meets your needs and the process repeats itself—over and over again.

The overwhelming majority of people I've met in this group (including the ones who "church shop" with us), end up spending more time searching than growing in their relationship with God.

Option C gets a lot of interest too, but Jesus said, in Matthew 7:26-27, that if we hear His words but don't actually put them into practice, we're like a man who builds his house on the sand. When the inevitable rain falls and the wind blows, our house comes crashing down.

The problem with options A, B, and C is that we separate ourselves as the decision maker. The Bible is not unclear in detailing the problems with this strategy.

Proverbs 18:1 warns us, "He who separates himself seeks his own desire; he quarrels against all sound wisdom" (NASB). In case you're wondering, in the original Hebrew, the word "all" means "*all.*" In other words, every piece of dependable, logical, proven, trustworthy wisdom shouts to us, "Don't do it!"

The ESV translates the second half of the verse, "he breaks out against all sound judgment." If sound judgment is like a protective wall keeping the good parts of our decision-making in and the bad parts out, then separating ourselves from the source of wisdom is like taking a jackhammer and breaking down the very thing protecting us from danger.

A common mistake people often make early in their spiritual development is to think, *It's me and Jesus. That's what really matters.*

In our radically individualistic, consumer-driven culture, it's easy to view this as a freedom that will make our lives better. But it's not true.

Jesus said that starting a genuine relationship with Him was like being born again. No one leaves a baby on their own—it's cared for and grows in the context of a loving family.

Let's look at the two verses at the start of this chapter. I want to invite you to consider God's wisdom in Psalm 68:6 and 1 Corinthians 12:18 as I encourage you to choose option D.

WHEN YOU GIVE YOUR LIFE TO CHRIST, WHEN YOU'RE ADOPTED INTO THE KINGDOM OF GOD, HE SETS YOU IN HIS FAMILY.

I realize that many of us have had incredibly painful challenges with our natural families, so it's hard for us to accept, but spiritual family is absolutely one of the most significant blessings God gives us.

God loved you while you were disobedient to Him. He cared for you while you were His enemy. He loves you enough to have sent His Son, Jesus, to die on the cross to bring you home. Then after all that, why wouldn't He have a place prepared just for you?[8]

God knows the details of your life. He has a place designed for you to grow, and because God builds according to the pattern of family, that place is a church home.

You don't have to live this way. You can rebel against the place He sets you—but you will end up feeling dry, in a sun-scorched land.

This image is in stark contrast with Psalm 92:12-15, which promises that the righteous will flourish like a palm tree or a cedar of Lebanon because they're planted in the house of the Lord.

THIS IS SPIRITUAL FAMILY—IT'S A COMMITMENT TO THE DIVINE RELATIONSHIPS GOD PLACES IN YOUR LIFE.

Spiritual family is God's idea.

It's not a style of church. It's more than friendly people who are excited about their church. It's a revelation, a conviction, a biblical pattern of the way God builds.

When we look at a landscape of Scripture, God always starts with a family. Family expresses His character, His nature, and the way He builds.

First and foremost, Adam and Eve were children of God. Because of the centrality of the family to God's overall design, the enemy always makes the family his first target. He concentrates his attacks and his forces to destroy families.

Within a few generations, humanity goes so far off the rails God uses the flood to press the reset button. How does He start over? With Noah and his family.

When humanity once again loses their way at the Tower of Babel, how does God respond? He comes to a childless man named Abram and promises to be his God and to give him children as numerous as the stars or the sand. Abram becomes Abraham, and at the ripe age of 100, his son Isaac is born.

This pattern holds true with natural family, but it doesn't stop there. As the biblical narrative continues, God joins people from different families, from different backgrounds, and from different nations and gods and cultures together in divine, covenantal relationships.

The book of Ruth is this amazing story of how a family flees Israel in search of food and ends up in the land of Moab. The dad and the two sons die, leaving Naomi, the Israelite widow, with two Moabite daughters-in-law. The first one makes the rational decision to go back to her family.

But the other one does something remarkable. Ruth clings to Naomi. Naomi tries to send her back, but Ruth says, "Don't urge me to leave you or to turn back from you. Where you go I will go, and where you stay I will stay. Your people will be my people and your God my God. Where you die I will die, and there I will be buried. May the Lord deal with me, be it ever so severely, if even death separates you and me."[9]

This is more than needing a friend or feeling lonely. This is not a transactional relationship. Naomi was convinced she was going to starve and die. Ruth is using covenantal language out of a conviction from God.

God saves Ruth and Naomi. They make it back to Israel, find food, and connect with a man named Boaz. He happens to be the son of a prostitute God spared from Jericho. Against all odds, Boaz and Ruth end up getting married. Within a few generations, they have a great-grandson who the Bible describes as a man after God's own heart.

His name is David and he becomes a king.

Before he becomes a king, David is forgotten by his father and mistreated by his brothers. He saves his people by defeating a giant as a young boy. This makes the current king (an insecure guy named Saul) really angry. He tries to kill David.

But David finds help from the least likely candidate. Saul's son Jonathan is the rightful heir to his throne, but he loves and trusts God. Because of this, he has the same conviction Ruth had with Naomi. He makes a covenant with David because he believes David is spiritual family. His own dad mocks him because of the loyalty of his relationship with David, but he won't change his mind.

Hundreds of years later, God moves through a prophet named Elijah. He spends most of his life and ministry alone, until God brings a covenant relationship into his life through the form of his protégé Elisha.

These relationships bring great personal fulfillment, advance the cause of Christ, and change the history of the world. But they're also costly and inconvenient. They require a much greater investment.

This pattern is repeated over and over and perhaps is best demonstrated through Jesus and His disciples. Jesus loved and served His natural family (His mom, Mary, His younger brother James, and His cousin John the Baptist were all leaders in the earliest days of the Christian faith), but He believed His brothers and sisters included those who did the will of God.

On the night He would be betrayed, beaten, and crucified, Jesus explained what divine relationships look like. He told His disciples they didn't choose Him, but He chose them. He told them He loved them the way the Father loved Him. He called them His friends and told them there's no greater love than to lay down your life for your friends.[10]

This is covenant language. This is how God joins us with Him. This is spiritual family.

Because the disciples understood the importance of this pattern and had experienced it themselves straight from Jesus, this is how they built. When Peter preaches the first message, the church grows from 120 to more than 3,000. What did they do?

READ Acts 2:42-47 and answer the following questions from the passage:

1. What were the four things the first followers of Jesus devoted themselves to?

2. Were they filled with information and knowledge or a sense of awe?

3. Were they selfish and focused on their own needs?

4. How does verse 46 describe their hearts?

5. Did other people want to join them? Who added to them? How were they added?

This church wasn't perfect—God made significant changes to the way they did ministry all throughout the book of Acts.

But the one thing they got right from the very beginning was the idea of spiritual family. They genuinely believed God had joined them together in His family. Verse 46 talks about their glad and sincere hearts. This was not a bunch of fake church people acting happy. These were not people without problems, but this was an atmosphere where they were enjoying every day they spent with God and each other.

They didn't come up with this on their own—they simply repeated what they had learned from Jesus.

When Jesus was on the cross, He looked at His mom and then He looked at one of His closest disciples, John. He told John to take care of her as if she were his own mother. Jesus had younger brothers, but He knew what His mom and John were about to face and that they were going to need the comfort and encouragement only spiritual family could provide.[11]

The church was creating a big stir and the Jewish leaders and elders called them in to investigate what was going on. Acts 4:13 tells us that these highly educated religious leaders were astonished because Peter and John were ordinary and unschooled, but everyone knew they had been with Jesus.

This approach continued to spread. It became normal in the early church for Christians to call each other brothers and sisters. Family language was everywhere. The apostle Paul called his disciple Timothy his beloved son in the faith.

You might be thinking, *Okay, I get it. Church people are supposed to be nice to each other and use family language.* It's deeper than that. I want to make it as practical as I can.

What Does It Mean to Be a Part of Spiritual Family?

1. You believe God placed you in the family.

This may seem strange, but we don't choose our natural family either. It's a divine joining, not a disposable or transactional relationship. How you treat your spiritual family is a direct reflection of how you treat God.

This is why conviction is such a big part. This is not a top-down heavy manipulation or control. When kids grow up and become adults, they get to decide how much time they want to spend with their natural family. The motivating factors are love and commitment. The same is true in a church.

If you don't have a clear sense God placed you in your church, then you need to find out why. You're going to have a hard time benefitting from spiritual family if you're constantly wavering over whether or not you believe you're where God set you.

2. You discover and develop your gifts in the context of family.

Family is the most natural environment for growth and development. That's what families do. In a family, people find interests, receive feedback and coaching, provide support and opportunities, and discover talents and abilities. The process takes time and patience, but it also requires close proximity and honest relationships.

3. You use your gifts to serve the family.

In a healthy family, no one sits back and watches. You jump in and offer your part. You're in the game. You're part of the team. You can't do everything, but you're grateful to contribute whatever you can because you believe that when *any* part of the family wins, *every* part of the family celebrates.

4. You put the needs and the goals of the family ahead of your own.

This sounds like a guaranteed way to get less, but the truth is, our greatest fulfillment in life is found in helping someone else to win. Jesus said that the greatest is the servant, that it's better to give than to receive; and His disciple John said that there's no greater joy than watching your children walk in the truth. John was writing to a church when he said it because he was talking about spiritual family.

Discussion Questions

1. What happens to us when we give our lives to Christ?

2. What is spiritual family? Whose idea is it?

3. Have you ever experienced spiritual family? If not, would you like to? What has held you back from it?

12

What Is the Goal of the Christian Life?

Discipleship & Spiritual Maturity

*Go therefore and make disciples of all nations, baptizing
them in the name of the Father and of the Son and
of the Holy Spirit, teaching them to observe all that I have
commanded you. And behold, I am with you always,
to the end of the age. – Jesus*
Matthew 28:19-20 ESV

Follow my example, as I follow the example of Christ.
1 Corinthians 11:1 NIV

In a significant conversation, the defining moment is often known as the "last word." It's the final say. It's the conclusion, the decision, the agreement that determines how you move forward.

When it comes to the goal of the Christian life, there are almost as many opinions as followers of Christ. Depending on who you ask, some might say that it is "to be a good person," "to go to church," "to live a good life," *or* perhaps "to obey God so you can spend eternity in heaven."

But what if we let Jesus have the final say? What if we gave Him the last word?

The first passage listed above makes up the last words of the Gospel of Matthew. They're commonly referred to as the "Great Commission." It's not the "Great Suggestion." Jesus expects us to take this seriously. Before He ascended to heaven, Jesus gathered His followers one last time and gave them their marching orders.

He told them to go and make disciples. In order to catch the significance, let me clarify a few things about this profound sentence.

First, the verb tense of "go" is perhaps closer to "as you're going." It's not a one-time trip. It's not "go and make a disciple one time and you're done." The implication is this: Wherever you go, make disciples. And second, the reason you have to make disciples is because they don't make themselves.

No one becomes a disciple by accident. It requires intentionality. This begs the question, "What is a disciple?"

Most people think of it as a spiritual student. You become one by adhering to strict rules and gaining spiritual information. But more than a student, a disciple is an apprentice.

They don't just learn information from a teacher. They follow a master and learn to do what they do. It's more about what you become than what you know.

This is so important to Jesus that He says, "Go to all the nations, tell them to do everything I told you, and I'll be with you in the process all the way to the very end." It's truly a "co-mission." He wants us to do it with Him.

At this point most people think, *Okay, that's your job. That's what pastors do.* But there's no distinction in either Matthew or the passage from 1 Corinthians. This isn't something for a few elite, super-spiritual, professional Christians. It's for everyone.

Although in our culture "Christian" is the far more common term, the New Testament uses the word "Christian" only three times. It uses the word "disciple" 281 times.

Jesus told His followers in Luke 9:23-24 that if they wanted to be His disciple, they would have to deny themselves on a daily basis. He didn't mean your life would be miserable—He meant you were never intended to be the center of your world. This was the expectation of what it meant to have a relationship with Jesus. The idea of a casual, what's-in-it-for-me relationship with God was foreign to their world.

The apostle Paul gives us a clear, simple definition for discipleship in 1 Corinthians 11:1.

A DISCIPLE IS ONE CHRIST-FOLLOWER HELPING ANOTHER CHRIST-FOLLOWER TAKE THEIR NEXT STEP. IT'S THAT SIMPLE.

READ 2 Timothy 2:1-6 and answer the following questions from the passage:

1. What does Paul tell Timothy to do in verse 1?

2. How does Timothy know what to tell people?

---

3. Who does Paul tell Timothy to choose?

4. How many disciples are listed in verse 2?

5. What three occupations does Paul use to compare this process of discipleship?

Paul gave Timothy the same blueprint Jesus gave His disciples. The game plan hasn't changed. The strategy is still the same. The goal of the Christian faith is to make disciples who make disciples.

The great news is that you can start doing this today.

It's not about how much of the Bible you know. It doesn't require a family heritage of Christian faith. All you need is a willingness to keep taking steps in your own walk with Christ as well as a desire to help someone else.

This is why Paul stresses both strength in the grace of God and reliability/ faithfulness as key ingredients in the process. You keep showing up. When you slip, you get back up. You continue to trust God. This is the heart of discipleship.

The most common question at this point may be the most basic: *Where do I find a disciple?* If you're a dad, this is easy. They're in your house. The most important disciples you'll ever lead are in your home. Your children, especially as they get older, follow your example far more than they follow your rules.

But this is an excellent window into discipleship in general. Paul called Timothy his son in the faith. It also gives us a picture of how this works if you don't have kids. The same principle applies in your workplace, with your friends, or anywhere else you go.

THE HARDEST STEP IS CHOOSING TO GET IN THE GAME. WHEN A MAN DECIDES HE'S GOING TO TAKE THIS STEP, GOD BRINGS PEOPLE INTO HIS LIFE.

It reminds me of an old saying: "When the teacher is ready, the student appears."

The best way to make disciples is to find people with a willingness to grow and add value to them. As you love and serve them, you build influence. This influence creates trust with the person and a responsibility before God.

This is what makes discipleship different from other forms of authority or leadership. In a discipleship relationship, we don't draw the person to ourselves—we lead them deeper in their relationship with Jesus.

You can't do this simply by adding more information. You have to be able to actually live it. You have to keep growing and taking steps yourself. You never outgrow it. Discipleship isn't a class or a program—it's a person we follow.

Bottom line: Be a disciple—and make disciples.

Discussion Questions

1. What is another word for "disciple"? What is the simple definition for "discipleship"?

2. Have you considered personally getting involved in making disciples? How would you need to change?

The Winning Playbook

Character Development

13

The Hardest Person to Lead

LEAD ME, FOLLOW ME, OR GET OUT OF THE WAY.
— GENERAL GEORGE PATTON

ADVERSITY INTRODUCES US TO OURSELVES.
— VINCE LOMBARDI

Leadership is easy to talk about; it's really hard to do.

- It's easy to read a book about leadership; it's difficult to get your team at work to develop their abilities and increase their productivity.
- It's easy to watch a TED talk or listen to a podcast; it's challenging to get your kids to listen to you.
- It's easy for your wife to follow you when she's on board with your decision; it's a whole different ballgame when she doesn't see things the way you do.

Each of these situations creates its own unique challenges. But there is one person to lead who is more difficult than either the people at work or the loved ones in your home.

You are the most difficult person you'll ever lead. And until you learn to lead yourself, you'll never be able to effectively lead anyone else.

We don't intend to be this way. No one sets out to be a hypocrite. Most of us don't see ourselves this way. We have goals. We have a strategic plan. We have standards of personal integrity. We have values we aspire to live by. And then life happens.

We end up doing what we feel like doing—and our feelings are a moving target.

While most of us are quick to give ourselves the benefit of the doubt, the people closest to us can clearly see when we come up short. This erodes our credibility when we come back around to hold them to a standard we're struggling to meet ourselves.

This process is painful.

Some of us deny it. Some have a reason why it's not our fault. Some are quick to find the faults in everyone else. And some end up feeling so discouraged that we give up on standards and goals altogether.

None of these options are helpful.

But there is another option available: We can own our mistakes, ask for forgiveness, and move forward with a better plan and greater resolve. This is why we need coaching.

WE NEED RELATIONSHIPS—WE NEED PEOPLE WHO HELP US SEE OUR SITUATION FROM A DIFFERENT PERSPECTIVE. WITHOUT THIS, WE DEFAULT BACK TO BEING LED BY OUR FEELINGS.

We need the kind of honesty we see in the Patton and Lombardi quotes at the beginning of this chapter to help us see when we're the problem.

This is what healthy leadership is all about. This is how you lead the hardest person to lead—you don't do it alone.

Luke 12 is one of the best windows into Jesus' philosophy of leadership.

Thousands of people have gathered around Jesus to hear what He's saying. The crowd is huge, and they're pushing and stepping on each other just to get close to Him.

Jesus cares about the crowd, but He uses the moment to make a point to His disciples. He tells them to be careful not to become like the hypocritical religious leaders, because in the end, there are no secrets. Whatever you hide, what you whisper in the darkness—eventually, everyone finds out.

Then Jesus turns His attention to the crowd. He tells them that their priorities are all wrong. They're worried about the wrong things. They're worried about their well-being and their needs instead of their relationship with God. They're missing the fact that God sees and cares about all their needs, but what He wants more than anything is their hearts.

He tells a parable about a rich fool who tries to build bigger barns to store all his stuff instead of being generous, being "rich toward God."

Again, He reminds them not to worry. If God can take care of the flowers of the field and the birds of the sky, how much more will He take care of His children?

In verse 31, He delivers one of His more memorable quotes: "But seek his kingdom, and these things will be given to you as well." Remember, He's not only talking to the men who will carry on His work once He's gone. This principle is for everyone.

Closer to the end of the chapter, He gives another foundational statement on how God set up the world: When someone has been given much, much will be required.

There's a lot to this dense chapter, but if we stop and divide it into several major concepts, we can take away some clear, practical insights capable of transforming how we lead ourselves.

How Does Jesus Teach Us to Lead Ourselves?

1. Character matters. What you hide will be found out.

Luke gives us great insight into what's happening. Jesus is becoming incredibly popular, and you have to imagine the disciples started to feel like they were a big deal. And in this moment, Jesus intentionally leans in and makes sure these guys understand that their character was more important than their popularity. You may fool everyone else. You may fool yourself. But you can't fool God.

Every one of us is vulnerable to this temptation. When things are going great, it's easy to lose sight of how critical our character remains. Talent, relationships, and favor can bring us to places of influence, but only our character can keep us there.

Most men greatly overestimate their ability to keep their secret sin hidden.

They pour massive amounts of energy to keep up the façade. At the beginning, it adds to the adrenaline and the excitement, but in time it becomes an inescapable, exhausting burden.

The bill always comes due. What you hide will be discovered.

2. Spend less time worrying about what you need, and more time trusting God, because He knows what you need.

Men are designed to carry weight. We want to be strong, in control, and able to provide for others. It fills us with a sense of significance, but it also comes with anxiety and stress. When we realize our abilities are a gift from God, it changes the way we handle our responsibility. We recognize our control is limited, which frees us up to carry only the things God has entrusted to us.

Leaders worry because they carry weight. We live in a world addicted to worry. It influences our choices and limits our options. It backs us into a corner.

WORRY PARALYZES US FROM LIVING BY FAITH.

One of the most important decisions you make every day is to focus on what God has called you to change and to let everything else go.

3. Be rich toward God. Put His Kingdom above your own agenda.

"Rich toward God" is a powerful phrase. There are so many ways you can be rich beyond your assets, investments, and net worth. You can be rich in relationships, rich in purpose, and rich in peace. Money can't buy those things, but each of them is part of God's inheritance for His people.

But the only way to gain these riches is to set aside your agenda in order to serve God's mission. This doesn't mean you quit your job and work for the church. But it does change your motivation. It does create a new grid in your decision-making process. Jesus essentially tells us, "If you make it all about you, you'll feel like something's missing, no matter how far you go. But when you seek My Kingdom first, you'll get everything else you're looking for too."

You can't outsource this step to someone else. You must have your own conviction about your unique contribution to God's agenda.

4. Everything you have has been entrusted to you, and you'll have to answer for what you did with it.

Life is short. The Bible tells us over and over that a man's life is like a breath. The older you get, the truer this becomes. We don't choose the time and place where we enter this world. If you're reading this, you live in one of the most advantageous moments in human history. But because we're aware of other people who have more privileges than we do, it's easy to lose sight of the incredible opportunities God has entrusted to us.

One day you'll answer for what you did with what you were given.

God wants you to enjoy your life, to enjoy what He's provided. But when you understand your responsibility, you live with a holy reverence to make the most out of your life.

This doesn't mean you won't make mistakes, but it is a great reminder to continue to ask yourself how your life is adding value to others. It's hard for us to see this. We need trusted voices to help us. But you can only benefit from those voices when you invite their input.

Discussion Questions

1. What is your greatest challenge in leading yourself well? How would the people who know you best answer this question?

2. Which of the four principles from Luke 12 speaks to you the most directly? What are you doing to grow in this area?

Leadership Challenge

— If you have a hidden character flaw, make the choice to bring it into the light.

— If you're not ready to own it in front of the group, choose one person to be honest with.

14

The Character Test

A new command I give you: Love one another. As I have loved you, so you must love one another. By this everyone will know that you are my disciples, if you love one another. – Jesus
John 13:34-35

Be kind and compassionate to one another, forgiving each other, just as in Christ God forgave you.
Ephesians 4:32

If it is possible, as far as it depends on you, live at peace with everyone.
Romans 12:18

Jesus doesn't mess around. He doesn't clap when we dunk on a 6-foot rim. He sets a high standard. He calls us to greatness.

Look at this command from John 13. It's not a suggestion; it's a command: *Love one another the way I loved you.*

"Oh, okay, Jesus. Is that all? No problem."

Most people know the Golden Rule—treat others the way you want to be treated. Jesus doesn't stop there. He takes it up a level to what some have called the Platinum Rule—love others the way I loved you.

In the spiritual areas of life, the targets and scoreboards are often vague. It's difficult to find out how we're doing.

If someone asks, "Are you humble?" most of us will pause, think, and answer something like, "Yeah, I think I'm humble. I'm not the most humble guy, but I'm not the most prideful either. So yeah, I'd say I'm humble."

If they ask, "Are you loving?" we'd think about the people we care about the most. We're probably self-aware enough to realize we've made mistakes, but in general we support and provide for the people we love. "Yes. I love my wife and my kids, my parents, my friends . . ."

Jesus doesn't leave us in this ambiguous, unclear area. He makes it simple: *People will know you're really My disciple by the way you love each other.*

This is the character test. If you want to know if we're the real deal, if we're genuine, there's a way to find out. You don't ask us; you ask the people who know us the best.

According to this, if you want to know if I'm humble, don't ask me. Ask the people in my life. Ask my wife. Ask my kids. Ask the people who work with me every day. If you really want honest answers, that's where you'll find them.

Not everyone wants this level of feedback. Let me be clear: You better put on your helmet and mouthguard.

A couple of years ago I did a 360-degree evaluation. If you're not familiar, this is a leadership evaluation that solicits detailed feedback from everyone around you in the organization. It was extremely thorough and anonymous. In the spirit of full disclosure, when I heard some of the comments, I tried to figure out who said what. I was trying to explain why they said what they did. I was looking for justification.

I learned some things that weren't easy to hear. But I was no longer unclear about where I stood and how I was doing in my relationships. The test was not vague.

Remember, as the ultimate leader, Jesus went first. He made Himself vulnerable. He let people speak freely to Him and about Him—even when they were untruthful.

He wanted to give every person every opportunity to have a meaningful relationship with Him. He did everything He could to be healthy in every relationship He had.

And He calls us to live the same way.

Let me give you some good news: Jesus knows we're in process. He knows we're not perfect. He's not expecting us to be what He is. But He's very committed to our growth.

Jesus does not expect us to be perfect, but He definitely expects us to make progress. And according to Jesus, our progress, our character test, and our spiritual maturity are measured by the health of our relationships.

IF WE'RE GOING TO WIN IN LIFE, WE HAVE TO WIN IN OUR RELATIONSHIPS.

Every one of Jesus' followers dropped the ball in this area. The people closest to Jesus—His very first disciples who were entrusted with the responsibility of launching the Christian movement and leading the church—consistently struggled in this area.

The disciples argued with each other, held grudges, blamed each other, and fought over who was the most important. The Gospel of Mark was written by a man that the apostle Paul basically fired because he was tired of him.

However, this doesn't let us off the hook. It remains the standard. Paul (and the rest of the disciples) had his challenges, but he kept growing. By his later years, he'd improved greatly in this aspect of his life and demonstrated a long history of patient, forgiving, sacrificial, and ultimately Christ-like relationships.

It's not easy, but nothing is more important.

JESUS VIEWED PEOPLE AND RELATIONSHIPS AS A STEWARDSHIP BEFORE GOD. HE SAW HIS OWN LIFE THIS WAY AND HE EXPECTS THE SAME FROM US.

We can't blame our behavior on others. We don't get a free pass on how we treat people who hurt us. We aren't responsible for the behavior or choices of others. But we have to own the way we treat every person in our life.

Relationships are very difficult. They're complicated. We all bring our baggage—hurts, mistrust, painful experiences, unrealistic expectations—into each new relationship.

Jesus is not a stranger to this experience. His mom, His closest friends, His cousin John the Baptist, His siblings, His followers—they all got upset with Him, blamed Him for things, insulted Him, unfairly criticized Him, doubted Him, and in His humanity challenged His emotions in every possible way.

But Jesus loved each of them and continued to invest in these relationships. He wasn't depending on them to fulfill Him—He went to His Father for loving approval. He offers the same strategy to us.

We don't love people because of what they do for us. We love people out of the overflow of the love we've received from God.

This is what Paul is describing in Ephesians 4:32 (listed at the beginning of this chapter). We find the ability to forgive and love others not because of what they do for us but because we've been forgiven and loved so deeply by God. If we're not deeply connected and receiving from this source, we won't be able to give it to others.

Period. Full stop. End of story.

Our kindness runs out. Human grace has limits. Willpower can't overcome every circumstance.

A vibrant, genuine relationship with God is the only way to have lasting motivation.

The biggest problem with how human beings treat each other hasn't changed in thousands of years. You don't have to teach children to be selfish—it's hard-wired into their programming. Our nature causes us to approach every relationship from the starting point of "What can this person do for me?"

We're selfish. We do what we feel like doing.

And this one insight explains the majority of dysfunction in relationships.

It's the driving force behind your disagreement with your wife, the challenge you're having with your child. It explains why you get mad with your co-worker who takes credit for your idea. And it's the reason we feel violated when someone cuts us off or sits there texting during the green light, forcing you to wait another cycle before you can turn left.

With more than seven billion people on the planet, the world is still starving for genuine, healthy relationships. One study showed that the average person has more than 300 friends on Facebook but when the same group was asked, "How many trusted people do you have to talk about life's most important issues?" the most common response was zero.[12]

Every person wants loving relationships. Proverbs 19:22 says that what every person desires is unfailing love. When the Bible says that it's not good for man to be alone, it's talking about more than finding a spouse.

The longest lifestyle survey ever conducted was done at Harvard over a span of 70 years. They found the single greatest determining factor for the health of a person in their 80s was the quality of their relationships in their 50s.[13]

The point is clear: Our relationships don't just impact our emotional health or our spiritual health; dysfunctional, unhealthy relationships take years off of our lives.

One of the most common misconceptions of the Christian life is that the more information you know, the more mature you are. It's simply not true. It's a widely believed fallacy.

That's why it's called "the character test" and not "the information test." The most basic test of our maturity is the health of our relationships. This doesn't mean our relationships are perfect, but they are becoming healthier.

MATURE PEOPLE GENEROUSLY SERVE OTHERS OUT OF THEIR LOVE AND CONNECTION TO GOD.

Immature people interpret every interaction through the lens of "What's in it for me?" This leads to disposable relationships, selfish ambition, and unmet expectations. It's true whether we're at home, in an office, or at church.

If we're constantly changing our most trusted group of friends, it's a sign something is off. The proximity and intimacy of our friendships may change during different seasons of life, but when God entrusts us with a relationship, it's not meant to be disposable.

This is why we can go years without spending significant time with someone due to circumstances, but when we're back with them it feels as if no time has passed. This is healthy.

We all become like the people we hang around and listen to.

Our culture tells us our fulfillment and happiness will be realized when our world is exactly how we want it. Yet, the most miserable people I know are the ones who are consumed with themselves and who try to control everyone else in their lives.

This doesn't mean you become a nice, friendly doormat who does what everyone else wants. Not even close. But it does mean you conduct yourself in every relationship through the grid of "Did I honor God in the way I treated this person?"—whether this prompts you to smile and hold the door open, to lovingly confront them, or to give generously of your time or your resources.

This is the genius behind Romans 12:18. There are two qualifiers in this one little verse: (1) "If it is possible," which means sometimes it isn't; and (2) ". . . as far as it depends on you," meaning you can't control how anyone else behaves; all you can own is what you do—". . . live at peace with everyone." That's the goal.

Biblical peace is not the absence of disagreements or conflicts. It's not a weird, fake, "nice" demeanor. It's the presence of God in the context of the relationship.

Jesus loved us when we were unlovable. He went first. So many people think, *If I had some good friends, I would be friendly. I don't want anyone to take advantage of me.* This thought process will leave you frustrated and lonely.

You may be thinking, *That's not my personality. Normal people don't live like that.* I agree. That's why the only motivation to treat people this way comes from God. You don't wait to love someone who can help you; you love people because God does, and He's loved you so generously.

You think, *If God placed this person in my life, I'm going to honor Him by the way I treat them.*

This doesn't mean every person is going to be your best friend and you have to always be ready to give people as much time or as many resources as they want. Jesus didn't do that and He's not asking you to either. It may be a simple smile or greeting, the willingness to engage with the person and add value to them, or the self-control not to respond when you're provoked.

He's simply asking you to honor God in the way you treat them and to ask Him what He wants you to do.

This attitude makes you healthy, but it's not a guarantee to change someone else. And it doesn't mean you do whatever they want—this quickly leads to co-dependence, enablement, and resentment. But it has to be your starting point. Remember, you're not responsible for them, only for what you do.

Even the healthiest of relationships come with miscommunication, misunderstandings, hurt feelings, opportunities for offense, and all kinds of challenges. While painful, this is also the soil for relational growth.

There's a right way and a wrong way to handle this: You start with trust; you believe the best; you're quick to forgive; you don't talk to other people about it but go straight to the person if you're not able to process through it with God. Matthew 18 gives a clear protocol for how this works in the church.

Of course, this process requires honesty, vulnerability, and a lot of emotional energy. It's far easier to say, "It's fine," and ignore the issue than to deal with it. But you can't have healthy relationships without some measure of healthy conflict. On the backside of these moments you create significant trust.

THE CULTURE OF GOD'S FAMILY IS BUILT ON TRUST, FORGIVENESS, HONOR, AND LOVE.

These are more than warm words; they're life-changing values you have to put into practice.

We don't retire from this process. But as long as we see it as the expression of our relationship with God, we will continue to grow more and more like Him.

Discussion Questions

1. What is Jesus' standard for our relationships? What's the difference between the Golden Rule and the Platinum Rule?

2. What is the character test? Where do we find the motivation to live this way? What is the most basic test of our spiritual maturity?

3. What does Romans 12:18 say? How does this impact what it looks like to love people?

Leadership Challenge

— Healthy relationships require investment. Pray and ask God to show you three people to whom you can send an encouraging text.

— Ask yourself if you're holding onto an offense or have chosen not to forgive someone in your life (especially close friends/family). Choose to forgive them. Let it go. This doesn't necessarily mean you reconcile with them, but it does mean you stop viewing them through the difficult experience.

15

Shattered Dreams, Broken Lives

It started with a text message from John: "I have to talk with you."

We'd been friends for a long time. For most of those years, I'd been John's pastor. He was a man of character, a committed husband, an engaged father, and a successful businessman.

We communicated regularly and it wasn't like him to send this kind of text—especially at this time of night. As a pastor, you know this probably isn't going to be good news.

I replied to his message: "Is it urgent?" After I hit send, those three little dots started blinking. I knew where this was going before his message came back seconds later.

"Yes. Can I meet you at church?"

I explained the emergency to my wife, headed out the door, and climbed in the car.

On the way over, my mind was racing through the possible scenarios:

Maybe there was a challenge at work.
Maybe he and his wife were having trouble.
Maybe his kids were in a difficult spot.

When I got to my office, he pulled in right behind me. As he got out of his car, it became immediately clear how serious things were. He looked like he hadn't slept in days. There were bags under his eyes, and it was clear he'd been crying.

"What's going on?" I said as I opened the door for him.
"She found out," John said.
"Found out about what?" I said.
"About everything."

It turned out that a few months prior, John's business had been growing steadily but was approaching a major expansion to become an industry leader. Everything had been in place, but as the deal was being finalized, some financing had fallen through. This obstacle would go away once the new stream of revenue opened up.

Until it didn't.

I was aware John was leveraged to make this move, but I wasn't aware of how exposed he was. He kept that part to himself.

He was so sure it would happen that he'd exposed the future of the company to make the move. This created a level of stress and pressure unlike anything he'd experienced.

Everyone on his team had been working long hours. If the deal didn't go through, it wouldn't just affect him—it would greatly alter his wife's lifestyle, their home, and the college plans for his two boys. This pressure made him feel insecure as he wrestled with a level of self-doubt he'd never felt.

I also didn't know that the only relief John got from this pressure was the support and encouragement of one of his co-workers—she also happened to be attractive, single, and impressed with him.

One night, the two of them were working late. He told me he knew it wasn't wise, but he started to be honest and vulnerable with how he was feeling. That's all he thought it was. They were friends and she was easy to talk to. She understood what he was going through.

A week later, another long night at work ended up at her place.

Instead of providing support, this relationship was now the greatest source of stress and regret.

He'd been trying to keep it from his wife and his boys, but one of them had been looking something up on his phone and accidentally came across a text message they thought was intended for their mom.

And then his world came crashing down—the financial exposure, the fragile future of the company, and the relational betrayal. His wife and his boys would remember that moment for the rest of their lives.

Rock bottom.

Now in the aftermath of the damage, he was looking to me for help to put his world back together.

////////////////

I changed John's name in this story, but after decades in ministry, I've known way too many men who share a version of this story. The reality is tragic, but at this point, I feel like there's nothing in me left to shock. I'm far too familiar with how real these moments are.

When you get involved in the lives of real people over a long period of time, you experience the pain of walking through these moments with peers, young leaders, mentors, trusted friends, business leaders, and new believers.

The spectrum is wide, but the shattered dreams and broken lives are always very real. It's not a game.

People like to say, "All sin is the same." This may be technically true—all sin separates us from a perfect God, whether it's jaywalking or adultery. But make no mistake: The consequences of sin are not the same.

You don't blow up your life when you jaywalk. Significant moral failures always leave gaping wounds.

No industry is immune. Gifting and talent do not protect you.

Some of the most influential leaders in our nation have fallen—people you would think from a distance, *Not them. It would never happen to them.*

The problem is that too many of us buy into this lie about ourselves. It seems noble and confident: *That could never happen to me.* The problem is that we're all 100 percent capable of destroying everything we care about.

THE BIBLE MAKES IT CLEAR: "SO, IF YOU THINK YOU ARE STANDING FIRM, BE CAREFUL THAT YOU DON'T FALL!" (1 CORINTHIANS 10:12).

I'm not trying to manipulate you through fear, but think about it for a moment: What would it feel like to be John?

What if your family discovered your most glaring mistakes before you had the chance to make them right or get help? How far would you be willing to go to prevent ever having to find out?

How does this happen? Simple.

You end up in the wrong place, at the wrong time, ask the wrong question, handle company resources the wrong way, take the wrong shortcut to the right deal, and choose the wrong way to try to fix it.

You have the wrong conversation on email, text, or direct message, which leads to the wrong internet search and the wrong attempt to relieve stress.

Before long, the thing you hoped would make you feel better ends up being the greatest source of anxiety and regret.

There's no flashing light telling you that you're headed down a road that will destroy the things you care about most. If it did, few guys would walk down the path. But far too many do.

What do you do if you end up down that road? It doesn't have to be the end of the story.

The first thing you need to do is get honest, quit hiding, and embrace the truth. It's the only way to begin to restore trust, which is the only way you can move forward. You have to choose to ignore the desire to give into the condemnation and quit trying.

How you get to this point makes a big difference. If you want to move forward, the worst scenario is one like John's—you get caught. This violates trust and makes it difficult for the people you wounded to want to stay committed with you. And when you get caught, you lose most (or all) of your influence with them.

Either case is extremely challenging, but if you're currently living with the guilt of significant secrets or a double life, the best thing you can do is get honest and come forward for help. In many cases, this accelerates the process.

The best, and hopefully most common, response to these moments is to face the temptation of a poor choice with healthy boundaries and godly relationships.

If you want help, it can be done. You can conduct your business with integrity. You can honor your wife. You can be faithful to your children. And even if you've blown it, God is willing to help you build differently.

Discussion Questions

1. Have you ever known someone like John? What was it like watching him try to move forward?

2. What do you do when the stress and the pressure close in on you? Where do you turn for relief?

3. If you find yourself in a situation like John's, do you know where you'd go for help?

Leadership Challenge

— Identify the areas where you're over-leveraged (examples: financially, relationally, emotionally, etc.). This is where you're most vulnerable.
— Don't wait until there's a major mistake. Determine the person you're going to ask for help when you're headed for trouble.
— Become the kind of trusted friend someone would turn to in a moment like this.

16

The Power of Sex

There's a famous saying in advertising: "Sex sells."

It became well known because it's true. If you have a struggling product and you want people to pay more attention, surround it with sex. People are so fascinated with sex that they'll notice and remember your brand.

I don't have to cite a study in order to prove men think about sex.

Something tells me you've suddenly become more interested in this book. This may be chapter 16, but you probably flipped here when you saw the title.

I'm not surprised. God's not surprised either.

It would not be an exaggeration to suggest our culture worships sex. Think about the disproportionate amount of attention, resources, and energy devoted to an activity that makes up a microscopic percentage of our overall life experience. Consider the level of influence sexuality has gained in framing our identity as people.

Sigmund Freud was one of the most influential thinkers of the twentieth century. He was convinced that the sex drive was behind most of the decisions and motivations of human beings. He also thought that every sexual feeling was worth pursuing and that the only unnatural sexual feelings were those left unexplored.

Freud died in 1939, but even he may be surprised, if he were around today, to see how commonly accepted his ideas have become.

There's clearly more to sex than biology or reproduction. There is a powerful spiritual component to this aspect of the human condition.

The Bible has a lot to say about sex—about both the incredible benefits and the very real dangers that surround the subject. Sex is a big deal. According to Scripture, the way a man conducts himself in this area of his life goes a long way in determining the level of peace and joy he experiences on a day-to-day basis.

And in stark contrast to Freud, the Bible creates very clear, consistent boundaries for sex.

From God's direction in Genesis 2 to Jesus' affirmation in Matthew 19, the Bible draws an airtight box around biblical sexuality. The apostle Paul brings us back to both of these when he gives one of Scripture's most exhaustive descriptions of a healthy marriage in Ephesians 5:31: "For this reason a man will leave his father and mother and be united to his wife, and the two will become one flesh."

That's it.

This is God's definition of healthy sexuality: a man and woman coming together as husband and wife.

Our culture is constantly redefining the categories and insisting they're all equally valid, but God's opinion hasn't changed. The Bible calls anything outside of this clearly defined window "sexual immorality." In case it's still not clear, all sexual immorality is sin.

The Greek word for this term is *porneia*—you're probably not surprised to realize it's the same root for our English word "pornography." It's a catchall to cover all the things outside of God's will.

Christians are often accused of being either naïve and prudish or obsessive in their attitudes toward sex. Unbelievers claim that Christians either make too big a deal of it or have unrealistic attitudes about what's possible.

God understands the power of sex. He knows the disproportionate influence this can hold over our lives—especially for men. That's why He makes it simple for us.

Psalm 119:9 asks the appropriate question: "How can a young man keep his way pure? By guarding it according to your word" (ESV). If it were complicated, we'd have a difficult time remembering a series of rules. That's not the issue.

THE REAL QUESTION IS WHETHER OR NOT WE TRUST GOD'S PATTERN.

There's no gray area here.

"It is God's will that you should be sanctified: that you should avoid sexual immorality; that each of you should learn to control your own body in a way that is holy and honorable, not in passionate lust like the pagans, who do not know God" (1 Thessalonians 4:3-5).

According to the Bible, when a person has a relationship with God, they can and must control themselves sexually. It can be learned. Controlling your passionate lusts is both an honorable and attainable goal.

Let me be clear: Sex is a gift from God. In the right context, it creates generous, unique joy between a husband and a wife. Notice that this description is not exclusively tied to the function of procreation. The benefits of sex for a husband and wife exceed the joy of having children.

But when sex is taken out of the generous, others-first, loving relationship between a husband and a wife, it's very dangerous.

Ask a firefighter—the same heat source used under control in the proper way can heat your home, cook your food, heat your coffee, illuminate your room, and provide the perfect water temperature for your shower.

When a fire is out of control, it can burn your house to the ground.

Whether you're talking about the ancient world, Freud's day, or our culture, most of the discussion surrounding sex centers on the pleasure of the individual.

Lust is a toxic emotion for many reasons but perhaps more than any other, because it is pure selfishness. The driving force is the individual's unhindered desire, without regard for how these longings affect anyone else.

The Bible is painfully aware of how these feelings can grow into horrific circumstances of lust, adultery, murder, rape, and incest that destroy families. There are vivid and painful examples of each of these in Genesis—the very first book of the Bible. Over thousands of years, this aspect of human nature has not changed.

Biblical sexuality comes from a completely different place. Its primary motivation is to honor and bless your spouse.

Because these starting places are diametrically opposed, conflict is inevitable. People who object to the biblical approach typically say things like, "We don't need a piece of paper [a marriage certificate] to tell us we love each other." "I didn't choose these desires." "Who are you to judge me?" And perhaps most confused of all, "Love is love."

At the heart of each of these statements is the same attitude: *I know more about sex and relationships than God does.*

Some people would not hesitate to admit this. They're willing to shout it from the rooftops.

Others would hedge publicly but privately acknowledge their view.

But if you're a follower of Christ, if you want God's blessing, you can't sit on the fence. This is not an option afforded to you.

Hebrews 13:4 removes any remaining doubt: "Marriage should be honored by all, and the marriage bed kept pure, for God will judge the adulterer and all the sexually immoral."

Whether you're single, dating, engaged, or married, you're called to honor the marriage bed and keep it pure. It's no small thing for the Bible to say God will judge those who fail to live this way. But it's not because God hates sex or is mad at us. He understands how high the stakes are in this issue.

Sexual sin has the unique ability to decimate two things God cares about: people and families.

But even before it destroys families, it breaks down the person. It hurts us first. In 1 Corinthians 6:18, Paul warns us to flee sexual immorality because anyone who sins sexually sins against their own body—the very place God wants to come and make His home.

This is why sexual sin always carries an extra measure of guilt and shame. It's not God who makes you feel dirty—it's the sin.

That's why God wants to help you avoid the snares and challenges surrounding this issue.

Sex is powerful. Its influence is enormous in our culture. But you don't have to be a statistic or another tragic story. If you're struggling in this area, go to a trusted voice (for example someone in your small group or at church) and talk to them honestly about what's happening.

In 1 John 1:9 it says, "If we confess our sins, he is faithful and just and will forgive us our sins and purify us from all unrighteousness." There's forgiveness from God and help from each other. James 5:16a says, "Therefore confess your sins to each other and pray for each other so that you may be healed."

Don't try to solve it yourself. Get help. Come clean. The stakes are too high.

Discussion Questions

1. Is it difficult for you to talk about sex? If so, what makes it challenging?

2. What is God's definition for healthy sexuality? Why do you think this is controversial?

3. What does it mean to honor marriage? Why is this important?

Leadership Challenge

— Name one practical way you're going to honor marriage whether you're single, dating, engaged, or married.

— Name two practical safeguards you have to avoid sexual immorality in your life.

17

Unrighteous Appetites

I made a covenant with my eyes not to look
lustfully at a young woman.
Job 31:1

When you're a young man, it feels like you spend most days waiting for something important to happen. I distinctly remember feeling this way.

And now, somehow, I have children who have moved out of my house and are on to the next phase of their lives.

One of the things I realized over this process is that the desires and attitudes of men remain fairly unchanged: We want to feel strong, we want to accomplish something important, and we want the approval of those we respect.

And we'd also like to see a naked lady.

Does that sound crazy? Did it surprise you? Either way, I'm sure you'd agree it's true.

But how this particular desire takes place has changed exponentially since I was a teenager.

If you were in junior high in the '80s, your options were limited. Maybe your parents had premium cable and you could sneak a peek late at night. Maybe someone you knew had access to the kind of magazines they kept behind the counter. Those options typically required careful, strategic planning like you were trying to rob a bank.

Today these images come looking for men through the technological devices we have around us at all times. And the cultural attitude toward pornography has changed radically over the past few decades. It used to be a dirty secret no one wanted to admit. Today, it's viewed as a normal part of life, and it's common for people to view on airplanes and in public libraries.

As Job points out in the antiquated-sounding quote at the beginning of the chapter, the Bible doesn't share this view.

Remember from chapter 16, the Greek root word for sexual immorality is the source for the word "pornography." Simply put, *immorality* is a catchall word used to describe something beneficial being used in an unhealthy or damaging way.

The Bible is not prudish or naïve to this desire. In fact, the Bible acknowledges and encourages it. The best way to see a naked lady is to marry a woman and commit your life to serve and lead her. Despite what you see in the media, all the data shows that no one has more frequent and fulfilling sex than committed married couples.

That's one of the many reasons why the Bible says in Proverbs 18:22 that the person who finds a wife finds a good thing and receives favor from the Lord. This is the way God designed it to work.

There are all kinds of problems with pornography—far more than we have time to discuss—but the biggest issue is the way it fundamentally changes a person's understanding about sex.

It takes something meant to be reserved for the most unique, vulnerable, trusting relationship and transforms it into pure lust—selfish stimulation, exploited for personal pleasure. This continues to damage the individual after they've interacted with the material, altering their expectations and relationship with sex.

BIBLICAL SEX IS NOT LUST. IT'S NOT DIRTY. IT'S NOT EVEN PRIMARILY ABOUT YOUR NEEDS. IT'S A GIFT. IT'S A LOVING, GENEROUS WAY TO MEET THE NEEDS OF YOUR SPOUSE.

One of the most damaging aspects of pornography is that it cheapens the maturity and selflessness God intended as a requirement for an active sex life. If you love and treat your wife well, your needs will be more than met. If you mistreat her, you end up lonely on the couch.

And it's often there on the couch that married men start turning to porn, because it doesn't require the same level of character or emotional energy. It's not just married men either.

Across the board, fewer men are getting married, and fewer men are having sex because they've chosen porn over a healthy sex life, with a real person, in a healthy marriage.

The unpopular, and almost never admitted, reality is that this same demographic is not just less satisfied sexually, but they also have a much lower level of fulfillment with life overall.

Avoiding pornography is not an arbitrary rule God set up. It's toxic. It has the destructive power to damage the abuser and their ability to maintain healthy relationships, not to mention the damaging effects of the people trading their sexuality for money.

When a person is aroused, they experience a chemical wash in their brains not dissimilar to the process where photographic images were burned on film. In the context of a committed marriage relationship, this reinforces your connection to your wife. But when it's attached to a catalog of total strangers who consist of nothing more than photoshopped pixels, you create a whole library of imaginary images to remember and desire.

Like any other addiction, your brain begins to build a tolerance, which requires a greater level of stimulation. This is how the problem escalates. With drug addiction, your brain craves more. With porn, your brain wants different. Because of technology, there is a bottomless pit of unimaginably disturbing and deviant images to sift through.

Instead of this approach, you want to train the appetites of your heart toward your wife and your wife only. She is your standard of beauty. One of the reasons God wants us to save sex for marriage is that He wants sex and your wife to be synonymous in your mind. You don't think of one without the other.

If your wife is a brunette, you're not into blondes or redheads. You're into your wife. You have no "type" apart from your wife. She's what you're into.

This is one of the biggest mistakes men make. I hear them say, "There's nothing wrong with looking!" That's all kinds of stupid. Don't stir up any appetite you don't want to fulfill.

You don't flirt with other women. You don't check to see if "you've still got it." You don't send direct messages to old girlfriends on Facebook or send them a text to see how they're doing. You don't spend quality time with a woman who's not your wife. You don't have women up to your hotel room.

This may sound extreme or crazy, but this was Jesus' approach.

"You have heard that it was said, 'You shall not commit adultery.' But I tell you that anyone who looks at a woman lustfully has already committed adultery with her in his heart. If your right eye causes you to stumble, gouge it out and throw it away. It's better for you to lose one part of your body than for your whole body to be thrown into hell" (Matthew 5:27-29).

Jesus isn't playing around. He's equating the intent with the crime.

IF YOU'RE ENTERTAINING THE DESIRE, YOU'RE ONLY AN OPPORTUNITY AWAY FROM THE ACT ITSELF.

Think of how different this view is from our culture today. Our culture says, "Find the person who meets your needs and makes you happy." Jesus says, "It's better to gouge out your eye than to commit adultery."

Jesus equates adultery with hell itself. As a pastor who's seen far too many families destroyed this way, I get it. I've heard so many variations of this story, and every time it ends in shattered dreams and broken lives.

If you've made this mistake, my goal is not to condemn you or to make you feel unworthy. I'm keenly aware of how capable any of us are to fall in this pit. But in our world today, it's becoming increasingly common to treat all forms of relationship with a significant other as equal. People fall in and out of love. There's an online "dating service" intentionally designed to help married people meet someone to cheat with.

While I find this both insane and heartbreaking, it wouldn't exist if people didn't have the desire and the willingness to blow up their lives.

Both pornography and infidelity are massive problems in our world. But let me be clear: They can be defeated. Don't buy into the lie. Every man is not regularly looking at porn or cheating on his wife.

If you're going to overcome pornography and adultery, it will require two simple strategies:

1. Move toward healthy appetites.

2. Move away from unrighteous appetites.

Perhaps the most infamous sexual immorality in the entire Bible happened because both of these strategies were violated. Instead of leading the army out to battle as the king, David stayed home. He was looking for trouble on his rooftop and saw a beautiful woman bathing—she wasn't flaunting her beauty or taking a spa day. She was modestly and functionally cleaning herself at a difficult time of the month before her husband came home from fighting in the battle the king was supposed to be leading.

David was looking for something other than his wife and found it. Because he was the king, he took what he wanted. These destructive choices wrecked the lives of two families and continued to shatter relationships for years to come. His sons followed in his terrible footsteps.

If you don't lead your appetites, your appetites will lead you. Your passion grows where you feed it. This approach will work in every season of your life.

If you pray for and focus on your wife, your heart will move toward her—even as a single man. Having a clear picture of the kind of woman you're looking for helps you to keep your heart away from those who don't share your values. A young lady is more than a potential conquest or a good time—when you see her as your wife, or someone else's, it changes the way you treat her.

Move toward being a faithful, godly, generous husband who cares for and loves his wife. This reinforces the appetites you can righteously fulfill in a way that benefits both of you.

THE GRASS IS GREEN WHERE YOU WATER IT.

The second strategy is equally simple: Move away from anything or anyone that stirs up unrighteous appetites. If a movie, a streaming show, a TV show, a website, a social media platform, an old friend online, or a person from work stirs up unrighteous desires, take a step away.

Do a little detective work. What is the time and place you lose control? If it's on your phone late at night, lock your phone in the glove box of your car before you go to bed. Make it hard to make a bad choice.

If you lack the self-control for the technology these temptations travel through, get rid of them. It's not convenient, but a flip phone still gets the job done. If the computer, TV, or tablet is a problem, put it in a common area where everyone can see what you're doing.

Remember, the goal is to move away from the unrighteous appetites and toward the righteous ones. If you have a history with pornography, God can renew your mind and make you new. It doesn't mean you won't struggle. It may not mean you won't fall again. The enemy often torments men and makes them feel like they're incapable of change. The shame of a bad decision easily turns into condemnation for something you've tried to quit before but it didn't work.

But if you change the appetite, you'll change the outcome.

Discussion Questions

1. Is pornography something you struggle with? When/where does it usually happen?

2. What are you doing to retrain your appetite in this area?

3. What safeguards do you have in place against unrighteous feelings for someone other than your wife?

Leadership Challenge

— Choose one trusted person in your life (other than your wife) to be brutally honest with regarding your unhealthy appetites.
— Ask them if they'd be willing to help you.
— Commit to contact them when you're tempted—not once you've already acted on the desire.

18

The Spiritual Head of the Home

I'm kind of a simple guy. I grew up hunting and fishing in East Texas. It may have been my perspective, but it seemed like life was pretty simple back then.

When I went to college, I remember hearing about gender studies. I didn't know that was a thing.

Apparently, there were all these discussions and arguments about the roles of men and women. After finishing multiple degrees and working with people from all different socioeconomic backgrounds from all around the world, I have a greater appreciation for the nuances of this discussion.

Everyone's got an opinion, and most people are upset. Really upset.

They believe that if you can adjust systems of privilege and power, eliminate all differentiations and categories between male and female roles, legislate their perceptions of "fair," then life will end up as a glorious utopia. According to this view, the problem is the "patriarchy"—men and their abusive use of power.

I wholeheartedly agree that most of the problems in families are the result of poor leadership on the part of men. However, I don't believe the solution is to throw out the structure. The real issue isn't male versus female; it's good versus bad leadership.

Let me be clear: I'm a very grateful husband to an amazing wife, the father of three incredible daughters, and a brother to two dynamic sisters. All of them are gifted, determined, opinionated, and strong.

I have a vested, personal interest in creating environments where women can reach their highest potential. I'm not a knuckle-dragging caveman telling women to get back in the kitchen. But it's just as crazy to suggest there are no differences between men and women.

This isn't theory to me—I've seen what it does to real people and hurting families. Because I'm a pastor, I'm saddened, but not surprised, when we disregard God's Word and suffer the consequences.

A big part of the problem is perception. Most people equate the biblical model with a stiff religious paradigm they've heard horror stories about. The average person thinks Dad is either serious and emotionally distant or overly goofy with no real answers. Mom, on the other hand, is under-appreciated and always there to save the day.

So, when the Bible comes along and says the man is the head of the home, it sounds untrustworthy or just plain wrong. This has far more to do with cultural narratives and personal experience than the biblical model.

In the first few chapters of Genesis, we see the original intent for a family dynamic. God starts with a man named Adam and entrusts this man with gifts and the responsibility to lead and care for both the land and the animals. This responsibility is not a license to dominate but a call to serve.

God does not want the man to be alone, so he gives Adam a wife, and the two of them build a life together. They enjoy their home and spend time with God together every day.

This is the model for every family. The natural result is a growing, vibrant relationship between the husband and wife. What most people miss is that the key to a great marriage is that both the husband and the wife have their own growing relationship with God. It's all a gift from God, and the result is that both the size of the family and the joy, peace, and love in the family grow.

The recipe hasn't changed. God never changed His mind, but He also understands the challenges preventing us from this idealistic picture. From the first family to every other family since, human beings have messed up the model.

Because the family is so central to how God builds, He does the unthinkable—He sends His own Son to show us how to live and love each other. Husbands are supposed to love their wives the way Jesus loves His people. That's the standard.

WHEN YOU UNDERSTAND THAT GOD IS A LOVING FATHER WHO CARES FOR US, AND THAT EVERYTHING WE HAVE IN THIS LIFE IS A GIFT FROM HIM, IT CHANGES EVERYTHING.

As we've learned, it means we'll all give an account for everything we've been entrusted with.

"For the husband is the head of the wife as Christ is the head of the church, his body, of which he is the Savior. Now as the church submits to Christ, so also wives should submit to their husbands in everything. Husbands, love your wives, just as Christ loved the church and gave himself up for her" (Ephesians 5:23-25).

Someone has to be the head, but no head can survive without a body. It's a mutually interdependent relationship in which each part benefits most when it serves the other.

I realize "submit" is a scary word. In the UFC, a submission is a "tap out." You surrender. It's an admission of defeat.

But in this picture of the family, there are no losers. Both parties are willing to follow the mutually agreed upon terms of this relationship because they trust God and believe He wants the whole family to win. Both parties are subject to a ruling body. Submitting isn't fun, but it's far better than the alternative where there are no guidelines, and someone ends up getting seriously injured in a way they'll never recover.

IF WE WANT GOD'S BLESSING, WE DON'T BUILD BASED ON WHAT WE THINK OR WHAT CULTURE TELLS US. WE START WITH: *WHAT DOES GOD BLESS?*

The way God designed the home, each member is designed to honor and serve others. This starts with the head of the home—the man. He goes first. In other words, Dad sets the tone for the home. When he's engaged and serving his family, everyone benefits.

We see this throughout the Bible but especially in the New Testament as the message of Jesus changes the lives of men, and as a result, their entire families. There are four different places where this is recorded: (1) a royal official in Cana in John 4:53, (2) with a Centurion named Cornelius in Acts 10, (3) with a jailer in Acts 16, and (4) with Crispus, the synagogue leader, in Acts 18. The Bible says that when the men give their lives to Jesus, the significance of this change results in their "entire household" being saved.

Paul was so used to this happening that four different times in his letters, he sends his greeting to an entire household of believers.

When we say the man is the head of the home, it doesn't mean the wife and children have no say or they're stunted in their growth, vision, or development. Good leaders don't lead this way. In fact, when a man is leading with the power of the Spirit, everyone in the family should flourish and grow.

It doesn't mean the man is necessarily the most spiritual person. His wife or children may have more understanding of the Bible or may be more spiritually mature at this point in their lives.

It doesn't mean the man unilaterally handles all the important things in the home. It doesn't speak to the division of roles either—sometimes the unique gifts make more sense for the wife to manage the finances, provide the primary income, or handle the family calendar.

But what you can't replace are the spiritual weight and the responsibility. The man has to be the one to put his foot on the ground and say, "As for me and my house, we will serve the Lord."

When there's no consensus on a major decision, the man can't take a passive role and then point the finger of blame at his wife or children. This doesn't mean he won't make mistakes. But it does mean he's willing to take responsibility under the authority and covering God's given him to lead.

This includes the simple everyday things like getting everyone up and out the door to church, as well as more complicated decisions like navigating the kids' extracurricular schedules, potential job transfers, and big financial decisions.

When we understand this is how God builds, not only does it change the current leadership of a man carrying these responsibilities, but it also changes how he trains his children, and how single people find someone who shares their values.

As the head of the home, it's the husband's/dad's job to steward the culture of the home. This means he sets the tone when it comes to relational health. He's slow to anger; he's quick to forgive; he's not easily offended. When there's a misunderstanding, he believes the best about the other person and chooses not to assign motive to their behavior.

This also means he manages conflict in the home. When there are hurt feelings between siblings, when there's a misunderstanding with a coach or a teacher or, even more importantly, with the church family, he supports and guides the members of the family through the process of healthy relational choices.

I realize this sounds like a ton of emotional energy—and it is! But when a man lives this way, he helps everyone win.

Discussion Questions

1. What does it mean to say that the man is the head of the home? Who is the standard the husband is compared to in this role?

2. Is the head of the household a positional leadership role? Does he make everyone else follow his personal preferences?

3. How can you tell when a man is leading his home well?

Leadership Challenge

— List one specific area of your life where you're leading well as the head of the household.

— List an area where you need to grow in your head-of-household responsibilities. Name one practical change you plan to make.

19

How to Lead in Your Marriage

Getting married is easy. In fact, it has never been easier. All you need is a willing party.

Because of the internet, it seems like anyone can be certified to perform a ceremony—Elvis impersonators, people who haven't finished high school, a single guy in his 30s who plays video games 10 hours a day.

And yet, fewer people are getting married than ever before. It's easy to get married; it's much harder to stay married—and harder still to enjoy your marriage more and more every day.

The prevailing view is that marriage is a happiness contract. Two star-crossed "soul mates" find each other and remain in love as long as they meet all of each other's emotional and physical needs and make each other happy. Apparently, this approach works in your average romantic comedy—but not in real life.

Many people are deciding they don't need a ceremony or a marriage certificate to give it a shot. One study showed that 76 percent of couples live together before getting married.[14] This approach is in stark contrast to the biblical picture.

GOD CREATED MARRIAGE AS A COVENANT, NOT A CONTRACT.

Contracts are carefully negotiated to protect interests through limiting exposure while ensuring maximum gain. Contracts are created expecting to be contested—as long as you do this, I will do that. When you fail to meet this standard, our agreement has ended.

A covenant is something altogether different. A covenant is relational by nature. It's a generous promise we make to God intended to bless the other party at the expense of self. God is a covenant-keeping God—so when He tells us marriage is a picture of the relationship between Jesus and the Church, we understand a contract can't live up to such a lofty standard.

In order for a husband to live up to this, he has to go first. He doesn't love his wife because she lives up to her end of the bargain—he does it out of obedience to God.

This is counterintuitive. It's not natural to us. It won't happen on its own. You have to get your heart and your mind around this paradigm. And then you have to intentionally put it into practice.

Being a husband is like tending a garden. You can't put it off for six months and then try to do it all at once. You have to be present and engaged every day. And like a garden, you get what you plant. If you plant tomato seeds and nurture the soil with water and care, you get tomatoes.

If you plant spinach, you get spinach.
If you plant carrots, you get carrots.
If you plant nothing, you get . . . weeds.

Those weeds are out there looking for a home. If you don't tend the garden, they'll come in so strong that they'll choke everything else out. The same is true in a marriage. Seeds of mistrust, loneliness, discouragement, insecurity, comparison, and envy are blowing all over our culture looking for fertile soil.

Husbands and wives need connection. Connection requires both time and energy, and in our busy, over-scheduled lives, we often don't have what it takes to maintain this connection. If we're not careful, we retreat into the individual areas of our lives looking for margin, and our connection fades.

This is why I recommend some built-in routines—a morning connection over coffee, a weekly lunch date or date night, a brief time of prayer before bed, an annual getaway with just the two of you. This looks different in different seasons of life, but it's critical in every season. You have to prioritize connecting in your relationship. That's not her job—it's yours.

If your days are full, I recommend checking in via text, phone, or even email throughout the day so that you're not starting from scratch when you walk in the door. It makes a big difference.

Key moments go a long way in strengthening your connection. When you come home from work, take a deep breath, get off the phone, and walk in ready to give your full attention and emotional connection to your wife. This communicates value and importance to her.

More often than not with men, the connection need is physical and then emotional. For most women, a strong emotional connection leads to a physical expression.

When a guy gets a loving text from his wife, he thinks, *Things are looking good for later!* And when a wife gets an encouraging note from her husband while he's at work, she thinks, *We're putting the kids down early tonight.*

Back to the gardening metaphor, women take what you give them and multiply it. This is true physically, emotionally, and spiritually.

If you give her a budget and a physical structure, she'll give you a home. If you give her the right ingredients, she'll make an incredible meal. Or if she's a professional leading in the workplace, she'll find the right people to help her get the job done at home.

If you give your wife biological seed at the right time of the month, she'll multiply it into a new life. *Surprise!*

The same is true emotionally and spiritually. If you give your wife stress, short bursts of anger, and harsh words, she'll multiply it and give it back. But if you pray for her, remind her of what the Word says, and encourage her, she'll multiply it and give it back.

This is difficult for most couples to understand. Before they put themselves out there emotionally or spiritually, they want to know how their spouse will reciprocate. But 1 Peter 3 makes it clear that this approach is backward.

Peter tells wives they don't need words to impact their husbands; they can win them over through the power of their loving example. In the same passage, he tells husbands to be considerate of their wives or their prayers will be hindered. That's fairly strong. It's like God's telling us, "Before you ask Me for help, ask yourself if you're taking care of your wife!"

Unfortunately, this intimidates some men because they have the wrong mental picture. You don't have to become a pastor to lead your wife spiritually. However, I think it's interesting that God sees this as so important that He made leading your wife one of the primary qualifications for becoming a pastor.

Leading your wife doesn't mean you know more about the Bible, you're more spiritually mature, or you always have the right answer.

It means you're willing to step up and pray for her and with her, you're committed to growing in your relationship with Jesus, and you expect God to speak to you about your family.

As an added benefit, I've found that, without fail, when a man lives this way, he becomes much more attractive to his wife.

If you'll turn off the TV, put down your phone/tablet/computer, take her by the hand and consistently spend two or three minutes praying with her, it will change your relationship.

It seems so small, but it makes a big impact.

Colossians 3:18 instructs wives to submit to their husbands as is fitting in the Lord. It's hard for a woman to do this when the man isn't leading. But the key phrase is "fitting in the Lord."

A godly wife doesn't follow you because you're the man; she follows out of her love and commitment to God. Your authority is borrowed from Him, which means you'll give an account for how you lead.

This explains why verse 19 commands husbands to love their wives and not to be harsh with them. In other words, she's multiplying and giving back what you're giving her. If you don't like what you're getting, don't worry about her; focus on what you're giving.

UNITY OF THE HOME IS BASED ON A SPIRITUAL CONNECTION THAT COMES FROM A COVENANT.

This happens when both the husband and the wife start from this place in their heart: "I love you with the love I receive from God, not the love you've earned or deserved."

As we turn to parenting, I want you to remember that there's a reason we started with talking about marriage.

In my experience both as a pastor and as a parent, if you really made me summarize things, if you were interviewing me and wanted me to give you the most critical ingredient for success, here's what I've found:

Outside of God and His Word, there's nothing more important you can build on than the unity between Mom and Dad.

Discussion Questions

1. What's the difference between a contract and a covenant? Who do we first make a covenant with?

2. How is being a husband like tending a garden?

3. What does it practically look like for a husband to lead his wife?

Leadership Challenge

— Develop or strengthen your daily connections with your wife.
— Put your phone down and give your full attention to your wife each day when you get home from work.
— Accept the challenge to pray with your wife at least three times this week.

20

How to Lead Your Kids When They're Small

Children form their earliest impressions of God based on their relationship with their earthly fathers.

No pressure.

We care so much about our kids that it's hard for us to put it into words. Our connection with our children is supernatural. God puts something deep within us that inspires us to do whatever it takes to care for these little people. This is both incredibly fulfilling and a little scary.

I'll never forget coming home from the hospital wondering, *Are we qualified to take care of this little human?* Of course, it was only the first of many times I would have this feeling.

Once they're scooting, crawling, and moving around, we experience the joy of watching their unique, God-given personalities emerge. It's fascinating and often hilarious.

By the time they're two, they're laughing and giggling as you turn their spoon into an airplane. You think they're the cutest thing to ever walk on the planet—until 10 seconds later when they pick up their bowl, look you right in the eyes, and laugh as they dump it on the floor.

Not funny.

It doesn't take long to discover that they don't automatically do what we tell them. They don't come preprogrammed to do what's right. As much as they require provision, protection, and nourishment, they also require discipline. And the problem with giving your children discipline is that it requires discipline from you—especially when you're tired and worn out at the end of a long day.

"Do not withhold discipline from a child; if you punish them with the rod, they will not die" (Proverbs 23:13).

The writer of this passage was clearly a parent; his children must've cried and complained they were going to die after being disciplined, only to be fine a few moments later. I can relate—*both as a father and as a son!*

DISCIPLINE REQUIRES A TEAM APPROACH.

Mom and Dad have to be on the same team. The moment your children sniff out any separation between the two of you, you're in trouble. Kids have this innate ability to pit you against each other—sometimes they don't even realize it. They'll do whatever it takes to get what they want.

Mom and Dad need to say the same thing. If you don't see things the same way in a situation involving the kids, talk about it away from them first in order to maintain a unified voice. There's one team and one vision. One parent isn't the discipline parent while the other is the fun parent. This creates problems and imbalance in the relationship.

As amazing as your children may be, the world does not revolve around them. This is where our contribution of loving discipline helps them relate to others in a healthy way. Without this understanding, they'll struggle to relate to God.

Hebrews 12:5b-6 quotes Proverbs 3:11-12 to make this clear: "My child, don't make light of the Lord's discipline, and don't give up when he corrects you. For the Lord disciplines those he loves, and he punishes each one he accepts as his child" (Hebrews 12:5b-6, NLT).

Most children will initially interpret discipline as disapproval or rejection instead of what the Bible calls it: an expression of love. This won't just happen. You have to be consistent. You have to be clear. You have to communicate. If you do this, eventually they'll receive it for what it is, and when they have their own kids, they'll thank you for it.

So how does the process of discipline work? Every family has their own unique way of applying it and their own particular points of emphasis, but here are some of the basic foundations everyone should include.

1. Complete, first-time obedience is always the standard.
In our home, we like to say, "Slow obedience is no obedience." In other words, if you don't respond right away, you missed it. We don't issue threats. We don't count to three or five. We don't do half of what's expected and think it's good enough.

2. Always tell the truth.
In our house, if you lie, you will be disciplined. It's a nonnegotiable, because it erodes trust. Trust is the most valuable commodity in any relationship. If you don't set this foundation early in your relationship with your children, it creates massive problems moving forward. Even when it's awkward or uncomfortable for you—and there *will be* times—you want your kids to love the truth. It's vital. If you can foster it when your kids are small, then when they are teenagers—and the stakes are higher—they'll feel more comfortable sharing with you honestly.

3. Discipline always focuses on the heart, not on outcomes.

If you do the right thing with the wrong attitude, you're wrong. This is a classic toddler move. You tell them to sit down, and they do it, but you know they're standing up on the inside. They do what you ask, but their hearts aren't with you. This is a problem. It sets up a dangerous precedent of behavior modification instead of heart change.

We're not just parenting for behavior modification; we're parenting and training their hearts.

They can't control accidents and mistakes, but they're the only ones who can control their attitudes. You want to cultivate healthy attitudes (gratitude, thoughtfulness, positivity) and confront unhealthy ones (whining, yelling/fits, being rude, self-pity, rebellion).

Every kid struggles with controlling their attitude. They make bad choices. They lose their self-control. They get loud and squirrelly. They lash out in emotion. A big part of your job as their dad is to adjust their attitude.

"Foolishness is bound up in the heart of a child; The rod of discipline will remove it far from him" (Proverbs 22:15, NASB).

Discipline and loving correction are the processes by which your kids get their attitudes under control. It takes consistency over the years, but it's so important. You love your kids. I love my kids. But for someone else to love them, our kids have to learn how to control their emotions and deal with their attitudes.

Doing this isn't easy, but this window of time is critical. The investments you make in your kids when they are small pay dividends later.

4. Discipline is a four-step process: confession, consequences, forgiveness, restoration.

When they disobey, they have to admit what they did. Then they accept the consequences. Then they ask forgiveness for what they did—both to the person they disobeyed/hurt and to God. Finally, you forgive them, accept them, and help them see the difference between who they are and the choice they made.

There's nothing like a dad who looks at his child and tells them, "You made a choice, but that's not who you are. I forgive you, and I love you. I know you're going to be a person who makes good choices because that's who God created you to be."

It's often very difficult to keep your emotions in check depending upon the poor choice your child made, but you don't want to be upset or reactionary in this moment. We all can lose it and start yelling, but it overshadows the rest of the process. You want to be firm but calm.

IT'S NOT EASY TO BE REJECTED BY YOUR KIDS, BUT AS THEY WORK THROUGH THIS PROCESS, YOU HAVE TO REMEMBER THAT YOUR APPROVAL COMES FROM GOD—NOT FROM YOUR KIDS.

The process should soften their hearts, shape their attitudes, and turn them toward God. This is your job as their dad: to help them recognize and understand the presence and voice of God. They take their cues from you. You don't have to be a pastor or a Bible scholar. You just need to model it for them.

When they know you're responsible to the Lord for how you lead and care for them, it changes the nature of your relationship.

It gives your words weight. When you encourage them and tell them you're proud of them, it means more from you than anyone else. They want this approval. They need it.

I'm the kind of person who wants to inspire greatness in people. But this vision has always been bigger in my home. If I couldn't do it for them, why would anyone else care? I came up with this saying, and I really believe it: *You don't have to wait to be great. You can be a great kid.*

Here's what I've learned: If you tell them this, they'll believe it. They'll dream big dreams; they'll pray big prayers; they'll ask big things of a big God.

When they do this with a great attitude and respond well to correction, you'll know you're doing your part.

Discussion Questions

1. What do you think is the hardest part of disciplining your children? What practical steps are you going to take to grow in this area?

2. Have you and your wife maintained one team and one vision? If not, how are you going to change the way you lead?

3. Have you been doing the restoration part of the discipline process? Do you feel equipped to do it?

Leadership Challenge

— The next time you come to a discipline moment, pay close attention to the restoration part. Help them see the difference between what they did and who they are.

— Send a text, a note, or tell each of your children something simple and specific about who they are.

21

How to Lead Your Teenagers/Young Adults

When your kids are small, being a dad is exhausting, but it's not too complicated. You're trying to keep them out of harm's way, you're making sure they have what they need, you're helping them develop character, and you're trying your best to fill their life with fun and happiness.

It's kind of like solving a puzzle: You discover their natural abilities and struggles, you get a sense of what they think is fun, you know what makes them anxious or afraid, and you help them navigate through their childhood.

And then everything changes.

All of a sudden, they're preteens headed to middle school. They hit a growth spurt and you don't recognize them. You think, *What happened to the little kid who just wanted ice cream and fruit snacks?*

It's frustrating and confusing. You spend most days hoping you don't have to use the phrase, "Wait, they did *what?*" Unfortunately, many dads check out during this season.

Some dads take the opposite strategy as they double-down on rules and punishment. They hyper-focus on performance—if their kid excels in schoolwork, athletics, and extracurricular events, everything will be great.

It's not so simple.

Teenagers' bodies are going through massive changes, and their emotions are all over the map. The guys get mad for no reason. The girls start crying in seconds. As dads, we understand this. We've all asked our teens, "Why did you do that?" only to have them stare back and say, "I don't know."

This is funny because most of the time when you try to tell them something, they cut you off and say, "I know. I know." Young people used to need their parents, a teacher, or an elder to give them the information they needed. Now they just Google it.

A generation ago, it was hard to be a teenager. You know this because you lived it. But it's different now. No demographic has experienced the downside of technology the way our young people have.

When we were teenagers, we faced peer pressure and stress when we were at school or out with our friends, but once we went home, we got a break. We could relax and be awkward without worrying about what everyone else thought. Today because of social media and the constant presence of our smartphone, we're always "on."

And, as a result, anxiety, worry, and stress among young people are at an all-time high. Being a teenager used to be hard—now it's become life and death.

I'm not trying to be overly dramatic, but this is a huge issue. When I was a teenager, I knew people who came from a tough home who attempted suicide. Recently, the Center for Disease Control said the life expectancy of Americans decreased for three years in a row for the first time since 1915.

It may surprise you to realize that the primary cause is the sharp rise in suicide, which is up 30 percent across every demographic. But the situation is so dire among young people that suicide has become the second leading cause of death. And what surprised me was that the largest increases were in high-income, highly successful communities and in Ivy League schools.[15]

This is no longer a problem reserved for struggling at-risk teens. It now includes the driven athletes with good grades who appear to be excelling in every area of life.

My goal is not to hyper-focus on one issue, but I think it demonstrates how important it is for dads to engage during these critical years.

We all understand that one bad choice during this season of their lives can radically alter their future. However, if they can make good choices with a right heart, there's a compounding return that will benefit them for the rest of their lives.

Every young person has three basic needs:
(1) Significance (Does my life matter?)
(2) Purpose (Does God have a plan for my life?)
(3) Healthy relationships (Will I end up alone?)

As a dad, your goal is to help them navigate these waters. You can't solve it for them or remove all the obstacles.

- You don't get to decide what their gifts are or what they enjoy—but you need to help them develop their talents.
- You don't get to choose their career for them—but you need to help them prepare for college, internships, and their future.
- You don't get to pick their spouse—but you definitely need to provide wisdom and guidance in the process to give them every opportunity to have their own healthy family.

Here's the good news: Despite what you may have heard, the teenage and young-adult years can be some of the most enjoyable, fulfilling, life-giving years of being a dad. It doesn't have to be terrible. It will be challenging, but it can also be amazing.

So how do we prepare them to navigate this critical season?

How to Lead Your Teenagers/Young Adults

1. Go around to their side of the table.

When your kids are small, you have to be the law. You don't want to use them all the time, but it better be clear you have the badge and the gun—you're the cop. But as they get older, you don't want to relate to them this way. You want to be their coach.

You move from being across the table, interrogating them like a detective, to going over to the other side and putting your arm around them like a coach. Coaches call plays, but the players have to execute. The coach can't play the game—they get the player ready. This is how we want to relate to our teenagers.

Great coaches go over game film. They don't just celebrate wins and grieve losses. They're always looking to learn. They point out good choices and correct the mistakes. Then they expect the team to go out and do it the right way the next time. None of us learn from experience; we learn from *evaluated experience*.

Smart players listen and learn from their head coach, but they also benefit from assistant coaches. We call them multiple anchors. As a dad, the youth pastor, the small-group leader, the other parents who share your values, and high-character friends all become great voices that help your teen navigate these waters.

2. Help them understand ownership and learn to manage responsibility.

We live in the age of helicopter parents (hover over kids), bulldozer parents (plow obstacles in front of kids), and even Navy SEAL parents (drop in silently and eliminate enemies of kids). This may make parents feel better, but it robs the kids of healthy development. There's a staggering number of Ivy League college students who ask Mom for a wake-up call every morning.

"Adult" isn't a verb. You don't turn it on or off. Your teen will never become a young adult if they can't handle or manage their own responsibility. Our teens want freedom without the weight or pressure it requires to experience this standard of living.

Teenagers have to learn that adult freedoms come with adult responsibilities. If we shield them from this, we're not helping them.

Let them enjoy as much freedom as they can while being a great steward of their growing responsibilities. If they can't manage their time, their schoolwork, their car privileges, their finances, or their phone, they lose those things. This may be painful for you, but it's vital for them.

FAILURE ISN'T FINAL.

It helps expose weaknesses our teens (or us as dads) don't want to acknowledge. If you save them from the consequences of failed responsibilities, you set yourself up to live this way forever. This doesn't seem like a big deal in the moment, but over a long period of time, it can cripple the entire family.

3. Help them overcome stress and anxiety.

Even science shows us that we all want to take the path of least resistance. Your teens want to be part of something great without having to struggle. Sounds good, but you can't do both.

Our teens have been told they can be whatever they want to be, and they live in a world of instant gratification.

There's also this American myth of the genius—the super-talented individual who's discovered and becomes an immediate success. It's not that simple.

Nothing great happens without a struggle. Once you understand this, you learn to embrace the pain and the challenge of hard things. We won't grow if we're always comfortable.

We have to help them learn how to manage stress and anxiety. Stress isn't bad—stress all the time is bad. Like you, they need to learn how to rest. How to turn off their phones and their technology. How to quiet the voices in their soul. But it won't just happen. You have to help them take steps.

My recommendation is that you have a strategy to be involved with your kids' technology. This should include implementing screen breaks, creating content accountability, and cultivating other interests for them.

4. Model respect and honor for authority, and call them to it.

Every generation struggles with honoring authority. Our parents and teachers are human. They make mistakes, and we see them. As long as we see honoring authority and respect for others as something they must earn by meeting all our expectations, we'll never honor anyone. In order for us to pass this on to our teens, we have to be willing to embrace this ourselves. If we complain about our boss, the president, and our kids' teachers and coaches, we should expect our teens to be disrespectful with us.

5. Train them to think like a leader.

One of the most important shifts in the life of a young person is gaining the ability to see beyond the emotion of the moment to the bigger picture: *If I make this choice today, how will I feel about it in two weeks? Six months? Five years?* This doesn't come naturally to young people, because it's hard for them to think beyond the moment. It was hard for us too.

The older you get, the more you realize life is a marathon, not a sprint.

If you want your teen to think like a leader and not a follower, they have to be willing to think beyond how they can get the maximum advantages with the minimum sacrifice. I've found that when young people imagine what it would be like to own a business, it changes how they work for the business. Honestly, this is a helpful exercise for all employees.

As far as we know, the apostle Paul never had natural children of his own, but he constantly compared being a pastor to being a parent. You may not be a pastor, but I believe you would agree with me when I emphatically say my children are the most important disciples I'll ever have.

WHILE THERE'S NO PAIN LIKE KID PAIN, THERE'S ALSO NO GREATER JOY THAN WATCHING YOUR CHILDREN GROW INTO THE YOUNG MEN AND WOMEN GOD CREATED THEM TO BE.

Eventually all of your children will leave your home. Once they're gone, the hope we have as dads is that each one of them will have the ability to hear God's voice and obey. They will have ups and downs; they'll make mistakes; but if they hear and obey His voice, they'll end up in the place God has for them.

If your teen or young adult is far from God, you're not alone. There are many people in this situation, and I realize how difficult it can be. Don't try to make up for lost time all at once. Stay consistent in your love for them. Don't give up on them. Keep praying for them and doing everything you can to establish trust and reinforce good decisions. Pick your battles wisely, and prioritize moments intended to help them hear and obey God.

Before we leave this subject, I have two more insights I've found incredibly helpful.

First, as parents, we spend so much time, energy, and finances on finding our teens the right coaches and tutors for every area of their lives. Unfortunately, I've noticed we don't always apply that same diligence to their spiritual development. People often ask, "Where do I find these kinds of mentors?" It's a great question. I'm probably biased as a pastor, but I think the best place to find them is in the local church. This means weekly involvement in services (both student and main gatherings), camps, retreats, mission trips, and whatever else I can get them in.

I don't say this as a pastor; I say this as a parent: *My teenagers have been forever changed by the impact of people in the church.* Of course, this isn't easy. And just like every other area of their lives, it forces you to set up rides and adjust your schedule to help them get what they need. But I promise you won't regret it.

Second, young men and women all wonder if they're good enough, if they've got what it takes. The transition from a child into a young man or a young woman is a big deal. Everything changes. But kids can't declare themselves adults—they have to be called into it.

When you gather the most trusted and respected voices in their lives (parents, grandparents, pastors, small-group leaders, peers, etc.) to honor them, pray for them, and call them into manhood (or womanhood), it becomes a moment they never forget. Inviting these people to write a note of encouragement is a great way to make the power of the event last even longer.

I know this sounds overwhelming—it's a lot of information. You may feel like it's way more than what you can do. We all feel this way at times, but don't give up. You'll never regret the time and energy you invest in the people you care about the most. This is not an area of life where you want to lose sight of the goal. Remember, they're listening even when you feel like nothing is changing.

And here's what I know about you: When you set your mind on something—no matter how difficult it is—you can do incredible things. Don't give up. You can win.

Discussion Questions

1. What makes leading teens/young adults so hard? Why do you think this season has such a bad reputation?

2. What is your most difficult challenge with your teens/young adults? What have you done to fix it? How could you respond differently?

Leadership Challenge

— Name one practical way you plan to go around to their side of the table for each of your teens in this season of life.

— Plan a manhood or womanhood ceremony for your teen or participate in one for someone else's young leader.

22

The God of Your Money

People like to talk about money as long as the conversation has to do with how to get more or how to spend someone else's. Very few people are willing to listen to you tell them how to handle *their* money.

God is not afraid of this conversation. The entire Bible is filled with commands, promises, and wisdom for how to handle your money. Jesus talked about money (or how to faithfully handle your resources) as much as He talked about any other subject.

Every one of these passages starts with one assumption: *Everything* belongs to God.

Psalm 24:1 says that all the earth belongs to God—everything in it, everything that comes from it—it's all His. In case you're still wondering, yes, this includes you and everything you have.

It's easy to mentally acknowledge this idea or to agree conceptually, but it's much more difficult to actually live this way.

We like to think we work hard for what we have, so we deserve to decide what we do with it. *No taxation without representation* is at the heart of the American story. If an outside ruler comes to take from us in a way we feel is unfair, we fight back whether it's the king of England, our own government, or our boss.

Most people believe you should be able to enjoy the highest possible standard of living you can achieve. This sounds so appealing until you realize this approach creates massive stress because you end up living beyond your means. Our kids aren't the only ones who can slip into an attitude of entitlement when it comes to the standard of living we believe we deserve.

I believe in the value of hard work, the promise of social mobility, and finding joy in the opportunities and experiences life provides. These are biblical principles. But we can't just pick those parts out of Scripture while we ignore the guiding truth.

WITHOUT GOD, WE WOULD HAVE NOTHING. NONE OF US ARE TRULY SELF-MADE MEN.

Every part of the process that results in our accumulation of resources begins with a generous gift from God.

- We don't give ourselves life.
- We don't choose when or where we are born.
- We don't choose our natural gifts or talents.
- We don't create the air we need to breathe.
- We didn't invent our brains and the creative ideas they produce.
- We can't manufacture the energy we need to make our ideas come to life—we require quality sleep and good food to make them happen.

Our responsibility is to apply the hard work, discipline, and character development necessary to turn these gifts into blessings. Not only do we receive financial compensation, but also, as we said earlier, others benefit from our contribution, God receives glory, and we discover fulfillment and a clear sense of purpose.

Whether you acknowledge it or not, whether you're a student, an executive, a part-time employee, or the president of your own company, what Jesus said in John 15 remains true: *Apart from Him, we can do nothing.*

We're not the first ones to be tempted to overlook this significant detail. Thousands of years ago, God reminded His people not to forget where their blessings came from when they were satisfied. Deuteronomy 8 explains how easy it is for us to be prideful and arrogant, instead of grateful, when we lose sight of the fact that our ability to generate wealth only comes from God.

It's so helpful to remind ourselves: *Everything belongs to God.*

While this underlying assumption remains constant throughout the entire Bible, the overall view toward money is often misunderstood or misrepresented. For example, because there is a clear imperative to care for the poor and to meet the needs of widows and orphans, some have suggested Scripture is socialistic.

However, Jesus repeatedly dismisses this concept in His parables. His driving motivation is not fair or equal distribution—He's after faithful stewardship. He poked at this human instinct.

After Jesus' resurrection in John 21, Peter complained about where he was headed in contrast with what John's life would be like. Jesus told him, "What's it to you?" Earlier, Jesus told a parable in which some workers served a full day while others worked only a fraction, and yet all received the same pay. In several other parables, He used the setup where the first servant was given one resource, the next servant was given five, and the final servant was given ten. When it came time for performance reviews, the master took from the disobedient servant with a little and gave to the faithful servant with ten.

Jesus is trying to get us to understand that resources exist to help us serve Him. The moment we begin to serve resources, we exchange the life we were created for with a smaller, more miserable version—no matter how many resources we can acquire.

Money and resources make outstanding gifts, but they are terrible gods. They have no power to fulfill us at the deepest level.

John D. Rockefeller was the richest man of his era and the first American billionaire. When a reporter asked him how much money was enough, he famously said, "Just a little bit more."

Jesus is not anti-money or anti-resources. Remember, it all belongs to Him, and He called everything He made "good." He just wants to make sure we love Him more than money. He wants to be first in our hearts, in our lives, and in our balance sheets.

The best window into His view on the subject comes from Matthew 6. In verse 19, Jesus tells the big crowd of people not to store up treasures on earth where things fall apart or get stolen. Then He says that where your treasure is, there your heart will also be.

It sounds poetic, but basically it means that if you want to know what you really care about, follow the money. We can lie to our co-workers, to our family, to God, and even to ourselves about what we truly care about. But the numbers don't lie.

If anyone is still wondering how he feels about it, Jesus makes it really simple: You can't serve two masters. You end up hating one and loving the other.

YOU CAN'T SERVE GOD AND MONEY.

Jesus wants to make sure we're clear on what He's saying.

This is one of the rare times in Scripture when He repeats a phrase in two different contexts. In Matthew, He's preaching. In Luke 16, He uses it at the narrative climax of the parable of a shrewd manager.

The word for "money" is an Aramaic word you may recognize: *mammon*. In the ancient world, this concept was more than money. It was an intense worship of material resources, a devotion to all the lusts and excesses the world could provide.

I don't think I need to argue that this attitude is still with us today. Billions of people worship money. More than money, they worship what money represents—the freedom to do what they want, when they want, without answering to anyone else.

In other words, it's their perception of what it would be like to be like God.

Because all of us are vulnerable to this temptation, God gave us a simple test to keep our hearts right. Considering that everything we have comes from Him, this request is not unreasonable. In order to demonstrate our trust and devotion to Him and not to money, He asked for the first part of everything we make.

Not a random, secret, or arbitrary amount—it's simple math even a child could do. While it's simple, it's not easy. It's a subject people get nervous about when they get around church environments. But let's get into it.

Let's talk about tithing.

Discussion Questions

1. Do you believe everything belongs to God? Do you agree with Jesus in John 15:5 that apart from Him, you can do nothing? What makes this difficult?

2. What did Jesus mean when He said you can't serve God and money? How can you tell which one you're serving? Is money inherently evil?

Leadership Challenge

— Read Luke 16:10-13.
— Write down Deuteronomy 8:17-18, and put it somewhere you will see it on a regular basis.

23

What's Up with the Tithe?

"Bring the whole tithe into the storehouse, that there may be food in my house. Test me in this," says the Lord Almighty, "and see if I will not throw open the floodgates of heaven and pour out so much blessing that there will not be room enough to store it."
Malachi 3:10

"Tithe" is a straight-up church word. In my entire life, I don't think I've ever heard the word used in any other context.

If you're not familiar, "tithe" simply means "tenth."

The idea is that people who love and follow Jesus take the first 10 percent of the money they make and give it to God through their local church to demonstrate their love, trust, and gratitude for His provision.

This is the incredibly practical test I referred to in the last chapter. Remember, Jesus warned the people that everything we have is a gift for which we will give an account. To those who are given much, much is required. He finished this discussion with a clear challenge: *You can't serve two masters. You can't serve God and money.*

I know conceptually it's hard to grasp serving money. Let's consider these questions: Do we trust God or money? Do we look to find peace in God or in a dollar amount in our checking, savings, or retirement accounts?

Jesus is not anti-money; it all belongs to Him. But He is diametrically opposed to us worshiping and serving money as the ultimate goal of our lives.

And unlike other parts of our spiritual lives, this is not theoretical or metaphorical. It's not ambiguous or unclear.

The math is the easy part. If you're older and you're doing well in your career, the numbers get big quickly. And if there's not much margin in your monthly budget, it seems impossible.

But it can be done.

Christians have been living this way for thousands of years—not all of them, but enough to provide significant resources to fund and fuel the advancement of the mission of God.

There is a wide range of opinions on this subject, and I've seen people manipulate the Bible in all kinds of ways to make it say what they want it to. I'm fully aware there have been improper appeals from pastors or leaders. Typically, the motivation behind these actions is the fear that God won't provide.

This only shows they're human too. Whether you're the one asking people to give or the one giving, we need to remember that *Jesus wants us to trust Him, not money.*

So, let's jump right into the most common objections and arguments I've heard about tithing.

Two Common Objections to Tithing

1. "The tithe is an Old Testament idea, so it doesn't apply to us today."

The basic premise of this argument is to compare tithing to other Old Testament laws, such as dietary restrictions and detailed instructions on clothing or worship. Because we no longer adhere to these guidelines, we're no longer expected to tithe either.

There are several problems with this idea. First, Abraham (see Genesis 14:18-20) and Jacob (see Genesis 28:20-22) both tithed before God ever gave the Law to Moses. In fact, you could make the case that in Genesis 4, when Cain and Abel make an offering to God, they're giving the first 10 percent (their tithe). The purpose of the law was to separate God's people from all the other nations, but tithing was less about religious protocol and more about a window into their hearts. Wherever your treasure goes, your heart follows.

The second problem with this idea is that Jesus affirmed the tithe. In Matthew 23, He's correcting some Pharisees who were making a show of tithing the spices in their food to demonstrate their self-righteous superiority.

JESUS DOESN'T SAY, "THE TITHE HAS PASSED AWAY." HE TELLS THEM TO DO IT WITH THE RIGHT HEART MOTIVATION.

I caution people when they try to lean on Jesus to get them out of tithing. When you consider how Jesus applied the moral Old Testament principles to people in His day, He exponentially raised the standard.

- He changed "an eye for an eye" to "love your enemies."

- He changed "don't murder" to "don't speak harshly to your brothers."
- He changed "don't commit adultery" to "don't have lustful thoughts."

If we apply this same approach to tithing, you're giving a lot more than 10 percent.

Throughout the New Testament, we see this expectation of generosity, especially toward those who are giving themselves to the mission of preaching the gospel, planting churches, and continuing God's mission.

If we take our lead from Jesus, tithing becomes a non-issue because it's the floor—it's the bare minimum of what we do. We want to move on to Spirit-led, free-will giving and offering far above and beyond 10 percent.

In his first letter to the church at Corinth, Paul tells them to do what he told another church to do: Set aside money every week in proportion to their income to give (see 1 Corinthians 16:2). In his second letter, he tells them God is able to bless them abundantly in all things at all times, so they will have everything they need, including the ability to give generously (see 2 Corinthians 9:8).

If we're still unclear, Paul tells his top disciple Timothy to "command" those who are rich in this present age not to be arrogant or put their hope in wealth but to be rich in good deeds and to be generous (see 1 Timothy 6:17-18). Everyone thinks he's talking to someone else, but if you make $50,000 per year, it puts you in the top 1 percent of global earnings.

He's talking to us.

2. "The Church cares too much about money."
This one has been around forever. It makes sense because many people (myself included) have had disappointing and painful experiences with the church. However, if the church is meaningful on any level, it would

stand to reason that they would address an issue so central to the root cause of stress, anxiety, and challenges in marriage and family.

But if we set aside the mistrust and pain of past experiences, we'd realize how unrealistic it is to expect any organization to function without a budget and funding. No school, hospital, business, or family can function without good stewardship. Remember, the problem isn't the resources; it's all about how we steward them.

No one understood the importance of healthy stewardship more than Jesus. He kept coming back to the issue over and over. Almost half of the parables He taught (16 out of 38) spoke directly to the subject of handling money and possessions.

A church is a reflection of the people who serve and lead it. If the church trusts God and honors Him with their resources, the church will be generous and a blessing to their city—through their giving and the attitude of their hearts.

If people are struggling with trust, one of their responses is to become fixated on finding out where the money is going. This makes sense, but it's not practical; and ultimately it's misguided. Keeping a watchful eye over all the expenditures doesn't build trust; it only gives you more information. Trust is given from confidence in a relationship.

Biblical tithing assumes that God owns it all and you're only returning to Him what's already His. As individual stewards of our resources, we give to God and trust that He directs it as He sees fit.

This is not to imply the church bears no responsibility for how they use the resources entrusted to them. I don't believe this at all. Our entire team works very hard to be fiscally responsible and great stewards of what God has entrusted to us.

There are more objections, but I've found these to be the most common. Well-meaning people with good intentions have questions. But I don't think this is the primary reason people don't tithe.

Four Reasons Why People Don't Tithe

1. They're conveniently ignorant.
Ignorance can be bliss because we're not responsible for what we don't know. If you act like you don't know, you hold onto the valuable excuse "Nobody told me!"

The reason so many people have a hard time with the biblical instruction to tithe is that it comes with conviction, and it forces us to examine our hearts to find where our trust lies. But this is the same reason why God made it so practical. We're trying to avoid what's going on in our hearts, but God wants us to confront it—not because He needs our money, but because His way causes us to become the best version of who we are. We're prone to nuance and excuse but the tithe is numbers. They're facts, and they're a clear indicator of our level of trust.

2. They're afraid, and it's hard to start later in life.
Let's be honest: We live in the most economically prosperous nation in the history of the world. There's a lot of money changing hands all the time. Ten percent sounds reasonable in theory, but when you put the numbers on paper, you end up with some sizable withdrawals with a lot of zeroes.

When I talk with people later in life who've never even heard of tithing, they look at me like I'm crazy.

I don't blame them.

The lie is that it's easier for someone else, or if you had a little bit more, you'd be willing to do it. Having more doesn't solve it, because 10 percent grows with you. And it's not easy for anyone. I've been tithing since I had my first job. I tithed when I wasn't a pastor. When you stop and look at your end-of-year giving report, of course you have the thought, *That's a lot of money. I could do a lot of things with it.*

THE TITHE TEACHES YOU TO TRUST GOD.

It teaches you to build faith and not fear. It's a great way for us to develop this trust not only in our hearts but in our kids as well. Every man wants to transfer his most important convictions to his children. The tithe is one of the simplest ways to do it.

For years I've heard people say, "I can't afford to tithe." I understand what they mean, but they're not thinking straight.

Everyone has a tithe—it's the first 10 percent. Some people drive their tithe, some people live in it, and some people spend their weekends in the summer in their tithe.

But the tithe is going somewhere.

3. They think they're more generous than they really are.

We like to think we're generous. There's a big gap between the number of Christians who think they tithe and those who actually do. Most Christians give a tip—a little gratuity when they have a surplus instead of the faithful, disciplined tithe.

4. They don't trust God at His word.

It's one thing to say God owns it all; it's something different to trust and obey, even when you have different ideas for what you'd like to do with the money. When some people consider the amount of money the tithe represents, they're tempted to direct some of it to a favorite nonprofit, a humanitarian project, or a worthwhile college or university. These are good things, but they're not the tithe.

Leviticus 27:30 makes it clear the tithe belongs to the Lord. Malachi 3:10 says to bring the whole tithe into the storehouse—a representation of God's family, His people, His Church.

Every person I've ever met who has even considered tithing has faced these four challenges. They're real, and they're daunting. Principles and willpower alone aren't strong enough to help you consistently overcome them.

So how do you do it?

Four Motivations Strong Enough to Empower You to Tithe

1. You trust God as your source.

Not your business. Not your salary. Not your investment portfolio. Not the economy. Not your skill set or your next big deal. All of those things are subject to change.

In Malachi 3, God tells His people they've been stealing from Him because they didn't trust Him, so they didn't give their tithes and offerings. God does something crazy—it's one of the very few places in the whole Bible where He tells them to test Him to see if He won't open the floodgates of heaven and pour out His blessing (see Malachi 3:10).

Most people miss the fact that the larger context of this passage is relational, not transactional. This is less about "If you pay your tithes, God will give you money," and more about "If you honor God in your hearts, you'll experience His presence and blessing in every part of your lives."

God is calling His people back to Himself—not just with their actions but also with their hearts. He calls the people His "treasured possession." When the people are close to God in their hearts, all the other nations will call them blessed. It's obvious to everyone that His hand is on their lives. This is the kind of relationship He's after, but it's only possible when you trust Him as your source.

Whatever you decide is valuable gains influence in your heart. If you genuinely believe God is your source, you put Him first. If you look to something else to provide for you, you'll evaluate God's love and approval for you through your bank statement. It's not a great strategy.

Wise people believe living off 90 percent with God's blessing is always going to be better than 100 percent of what they get for themselves.

2. You love God more than money.

This is not a vow of poverty, but it is a declaration of allegiance. You love God more than your dream house, your lake house, your lifestyle, your career track, your level of comfort, or your financial independence. God wants you to enjoy those things. He's not trying to make you feel bad.

Proverbs 3:9 says, "Honor the Lord with your wealth, with the first fruits of all your crops." To give honor is to put something in the highest place. This is a picture of the tithe.

THE FIRST PART BELONGS TO HIM. IT'S NOT YOURS—IT NEVER WAS.

When kids learn about money, they have it spent before they get it. They know where the first paycheck is going. It's the same principle. When we say we can't wait to bring the first part to God, we're demonstrating that our love for Him is greater than the things money can buy.

3. You believe God has more, not less, for you.

God is generous—even to those who don't deserve it and can't earn it. It's His nature. One of the most common misperceptions of God is to think He's zero-sum—that He only has so much to go around. According to this line of thinking, you may come to this conclusion: In order for Him to give to you, He has to take from someone else.

When you think this way, you may see every financial challenge as a punishment from God. This is very damaging to your ongoing relationship with God. You will struggle to see Him as a loving Father, which has far greater ramifications than your budget.

You will feel distant and disconnected from Him. You'll live hyper-aware of who gets what and your perception of fairness. It's miserable. You don't want to live this way.

If you truly believe God has the supernatural ability not only to meet your needs but also to supply above and beyond everything you need, then you'll be free to live generously. These benefits are bigger than money, but God's more than confident in His ability to provide. Malachi 3:10 is the only place in the Bible where He flat out says, "Test me in this." In other words, it's an investment you can count on.

4. You believe God's plan begins with His Church.
We've repeatedly talked about how much God values His Church. It's the only thing Jesus promised to build. When you see His Church the way He does, you won't see giving as an obligation but as a privilege, and the best investment you will ever make.

And when you prioritize the church and build what God cares about, you can have confidence that you'll continue to experience God's blessing and hand on the things you're building.

Discussion Questions

1. When you look over the common objections and the common reasons people don't tithe, which is the biggest struggle for you?

2. Are you tithing? If not, what is holding you back? If you are tithing, what's the biggest blessing you've received through the process?

Leadership Challenge

— If you're not currently tithing, do what the Bible says: Test God in it.
— Tithe for the next six weeks and see what happens—not only to your finances but also to your overall well-being.

24

A Generous Spirit

The goal of spiritual development is not to become a more enlightened individual. It's not to acquire more information or techniques. It's not to work hard and climb the ranks in order to earn God's favor.

The goal of spiritual development is to become more like Jesus. That's the purpose of discipleship. That's the goal of the Christian life.

And you can't become like Jesus without being generous.

You can't be mature in your relationship with Christ without being generous. You can't become the person God created you to be without being generous.

It really is that simple.

Jesus gave everything. He didn't hold back. He didn't give to those who deserved it. He didn't try to get as much as He could. He looked for opportunities to serve others.

Sometimes we hear this and we think this is a noble way of life we should aspire to so we can share with the less fortunate. Jesus said we're the ones who benefit when we're generous. He said it's better to give than receive.

This was hard for me to understand as a kid, but the more time I spend with people, the clearer this truth becomes. The most miserable people I know are not the ones who are working hard to afford a more comfortable lifestyle but can't seem to get ahead. They're not even the ones who are facing significant health or relational challenges.

The most miserable people I know are consumed with themselves, what they have or don't have, and figuring out who is to blame for their unhappiness. In other words, they're selfish.

The happiest, most blessed people I know are not the ones without challenges or problems; they're people who've chosen to be generous.

Selfish people always have a reason why they can't be generous. Generous people look for opportunities to be a blessing to someone else. We all struggle with selfishness, but we're all created to be generous.

I love how Isaiah 32:8 describes the mentality of generous people: The New Living Translation says that they *plan* ways to be generous, while the New King James Version goes a step further—they *devise* ways to be generous. What an interesting way to describe generosity! To devise a plan is to plot and scheme. Those are typically words used to describe selfish motives, but the Bible tells us that generous people use their imagination to come up with creative and innovative ways to be generous.

GOD WANTS EVERY ONE OF US TO LIVE THIS WAY. HE WANTS US TO BE GENEROUS. HE EXPECTS US TO BE GENEROUS. AND HE EQUIPS EVERY ONE OF US TO BE GENEROUS.

In the ninth chapter of his second letter to the church in Corinth, the apostle Paul gives us a deep-dive look into how this works. Paul was writing in preparation for a generous gift these people had promised and he was encouraging them to make the arrangements necessary so they could give cheerfully.

He reminds them that whoever sows sparingly will reap sparingly, but whoever sows generously will reap generously. But he's quick to stop them from reducing this to a formula. What God really wants is a cheerful giver—someone who doesn't give because they *have* to but because they see it as a privilege.

In verses 10-11, Paul describes God as the one who supplies seed to the sower *and* bread for food. You eat bread; you sow seed—both come from God. He encourages these people with the promise that God enriches us in every way so we can be generous on every occasion. And when we live this way, the result is that people end up thanking God for His goodness.

One of the most fascinating implications of this passage is the notion of seed for sowing. In other words, God has a reserve of resources only available to those willing to invest them. He doesn't give seed to the needy or to people who are hungry—both groups are important to Him and worthy of His care.

But He gives seed to sowers.

Bread is ready to consume and meets an immediate need. Seed has to be sown in advance. Seed takes planning, intentionality, and discipline. Seed has to be cultivated and nurtured over time. Bread is the end result of a process designed to meet an immediate need.

Everybody eats bread—not everyone sows seed.

You don't sow seed to meet an immediate need, and sowers never stop sowing because they're always looking to prepare for a future harvest. And unlike bread, seed carries with it the exponential power of multiplication.

Sowing and reaping is certainly a biblical concept. In Luke 6, Jesus promises that when we give, it will be given to us—not just a little, but pressed down, shaken together, running over, and pouring into our lap. Proverbs 11:25 tells us that a generous man will prosper and that whoever refreshes others will be refreshed.

GOD'S GENEROSITY IS SO MUCH BIGGER THAN "YOU GET WHAT YOU PUT IN."

It's inappropriate to reduce it to this. God gives His best. He gives first. He gives without a promise of return. Jesus told His disciples that sometimes we reap where we haven't sown because God is so generous.

He wants us to have this same heart so we can experience the pure joy of generosity and giving. He wants each of us to know the life that comes from generosity without a cost/plus analysis.

But for some, He goes a step further. In Romans 12, the Bible calls this a spiritual gift—the gift of giving. Someone with this gift has a supernatural ability to receive seed from God and multiply that seed to bless many.

I've had the privilege of watching this gift on display, and its impact is incredible.

It's less visible than some of the other gifts, such as teaching, encouragement, or leadership, but when this gift is operating under the power of the Holy Spirit, everyone can sense God's presence. As with any other spiritual gift, giving should not lead to preferential treatment or special privileges; instead, it should be coached and productively applied, because when it's in operation the results are significant.

Whether or not we have the gift, we should all be growing our generosity. If our great desire is to become more like Jesus, we should constantly be developing a generous spirit.

Generosity includes your time, your talent, and your resources. During different seasons of our lives, we have a greater ability to give out of different categories. We can bless others and honor God when we give out of any of them, but a generous spirit doesn't look for the most convenient option. Instead, generous people give freely and are willing to give, even out of the area where it costs them the most.

Discussion Questions

1. Can you grow in your relationship with God without growing in your generosity? Why or why not?

2. What does the Bible mean when it says God gives seed to the sower? What's the difference between seed and bread?

3. Are you more comfortable being generous with your time, your talent, or your treasure? Is it more generous to give from the area where it costs you more?

Leadership Challenge

— Make a committed effort to practice one spontaneous act of generosity every day (at work, at home, in your neighborhood, etc.).

The Winning Culture

Values

25

Building a Winning Culture

DON'T TAKE YOUR CULTURE FOR GRANTED. THERE NEEDS TO BE A CONSTANT RENEWAL OF VALUES THAT LEAD TO CAMARADERIE.
— MIKE KRZYZEWSKI

CULTURE EATS STRATEGY FOR BREAKFAST.
— PETER DRUCKER

DO NOT LET WHAT YOU CANNOT DO INTERFERE WITH WHAT YOU CAN DO.
— JOHN WOODEN

Wherever you find people, you find culture. Culture is the shared language, shared values, and shared practices of any environment.

Your nation, your state, your region, your city, your workplace, your gym, your group of friends, your family, and your home—they all have their own culture.

There are few things as rewarding as being on a great team with a winning culture—and there are few things as miserable as being on a losing team with a toxic culture.

As Coach K warns us in the quote at the start of this chapter, it's an easy but significant mistake to underestimate the importance of maintaining healthy culture.

WE SHAPE OUR CULTURE AND OUR CULTURE SHAPES US.

We all have a responsibility for the way we exert our influence on the cultures we're a part of. And the more authority we have, the greater our ability to determine and build the culture.

In his excellent book *Boundaries for Leaders*, Henry Cloud boils down this concept into two critical ideas. All leaders are responsible for these two things that determine culture: (1) what you create, and (2) what you allow.[16]

If you don't like your team, your organization, your home, your marriage, or your family, before you look for someone to blame, you have to ask yourself, *What have I created and what have I allowed? What can I do to make the culture healthy?*

In different environments you have different levels of influence, but in every environment, your contribution helps to shape the culture of the organization. You have to own this. In fact, you're the only one who can own your influence.

Winning cultures reinforce their values. I'm not talking about slogans on websites or wall hangings. I'm talking about what gets measured, what gets celebrated, and what gets reinforced on a daily basis—especially down to the smallest of details.

Your strategy is what you're trying to do. Your culture is what you actually do. Strategy without the ability to execute is wishful thinking. Strategy is your plan if everything goes right. Culture is your repeated response to adversity.

John Wooden won 10 national championships in a 12-year period at UCLA. He recruited the most talented players in the country, who arrived on campus with dreams of continuing this incredible legacy. Coach Wooden was famous for starting training camp the same way every year.

The first thing he did was meticulously instruct his All-American players in the proper way to put on their socks and shoes. He did not leave room for personal expression.

The players thought it was a joke. They were expecting competition at the highest level, and instead, they were brought back to something they hadn't considered since they were children.

This was intentional of course. Coach Wooden was evaluating their ability to take correction, follow instructions, and demonstrate humility. If they couldn't pass this simple test, they would struggle with the grueling challenges of a long season with championship expectations.

You might see this as micro-managing unnecessary details, but Wooden saw it as an opportunity to reinforce a simple cultural value: Don't fixate on what you can't control, but focus on the little things you do every day.

Winning cultures help each person find the *why* behind the *what* and then expect each person to be internally motivated: "Here's what I'm trying to do, *and* here's why I'm doing it."

As a leader, you can't answer that question each time you ask someone to do something, but part of your responsibility is to consistently remind them why what they're doing matters.

And the only way you can do that for someone else is to know how to do it for yourself.

You have to be clear on who you are and who you're not. You're not trying to be another family, another team, or another organization. You're trying to be the best version of who you are. You're not perfect, but you're growing every day.

When healthy culture meets good strategy, the results are explosive. In New England they call this the Patriot Way, and it can be summarized by three simple words: Do your job.

The simple idea is, I can't do someone else's job. I can't control what they do. But I can do my job. And if I do my job and trust that my teammates are going to do their job, then we put ourselves in a position to win.

Winning is the result of a group of people whose primary concern is, *I'm not going to let the team down. I'm going to do whatever it takes to help my team win.*

No one wins consistently by mistake. Healthy families aren't the result of luck. Growing businesses where people can't wait to come to work don't magically appear. It's not just the result of one insanely talented genius either. This only happens when a team comes together around a clear vision with shared values and healthy communication.

This kind of team is willing to make personal sacrifices for the benefit of the team—which ends up producing a much higher level of fulfillment for everyone. Individuals may score touchdowns, but only teams win championships.

A young man named Noah works as a barista at the Four Seasons Hotel in Las Vegas. Noah is funny and engaging—he makes getting a cup of coffee in a hotel a memorable experience. He loves his job. Noah explained that throughout the course of his day, managers ask him how he's doing and if there's anything he needs to do his job better. Not just his direct report—*any* manager.

Their job is to help him do his job. Then the whole team wins.

Losing cultures don't work like this. They're not sure who or what they're trying to be. Noah works another job that he doesn't love. The managers there only stop employees to tell them when they're doing something wrong.

Simon Sinek clarifies this in a simple and helpful way: "A team is not a group of people who work together. A team is a group of people that trust each other."[17]

THE NUMBER-ONE PROBLEM OF ALL UNHEALTHY CULTURES IS THE SAME: EACH PERSON IS OUT FOR THEMSELVES INSTEAD OF THE OVERALL BENEFIT OF THE TEAM.

It doesn't matter how talented you are. It doesn't matter how many resources or opportunities you have.

When the people on a team are motivated by selfish ambition, and they stop trusting each other, it becomes impossible to get healthy. This happens whether you're talking about a family, a team, a business, or a church.

Culture is contagious. We're social animals; we observe and repeat the language and behavior of the people we're around. That's why it's so critical we constantly reinforce and encourage winning language and behavior and challenge losing mindsets.

If you've never been in a winning culture, it's hard to know what you're missing. It's hard to keep holding onto the hope that something better exists. No one wants to go to a job they hate every day or come home to toxic interactions in their home, but if it's all you know, it becomes difficult to expect anything different.

Business consultant and best-selling author Patrick Lencioni believes the overall health of the organization is the single greatest advantage any team can receive. And the best news is that the team gets to decide how healthy they want to be.

Discussion Questions

1. What is culture? What's the healthiest culture you've been a part of? What makes it a winning environment?

2. What are the two things leaders are responsible for? Which one of these is more difficult for you? How are you going to get better at this?

3. What's the number-one problem with all unhealthy cultures? Where do you struggle with this problem?

Leadership Challenge

— Honestly assess your team at work. How healthy is the culture? Name one specific thing you need to either create or correct.
— Honestly assess your team at home. How healthy is the culture? Name one specific thing you need to either create or correct.

26

The Two Types
of Values

The integrity of the upright guides them,
but the unfaithful are destroyed by their duplicity.
Proverbs 11:3

Culture isn't accidental or arbitrary. Culture is the inevitable result of what leaders create and allow. And what you create and what you allow are determined by what you value.

Values shape culture and help you prioritize. They form decisions, guide strategy, create the grid for discipline and conflict management, and attract certain types of people while repelling others.

Organizations and leaders can find themselves in the awkward position of seeing themselves differently from the way everyone else views them. Often, they're the last to know.

Every retail business will say they value customer service. They'll put it on their website and mission statement. But you'll find out what they really value when you have a problem.

Every school will champion the value of education. They'll point to metrics to demonstrate their success. But until you have clarity on how they measure and evaluate their progress, you may be surprised by what they prioritize.

Every church will tell you they value the Bible and serving people, but you don't find out whether this is true until you actually get in the environment and discover where they place their resources and emphasis.

Every organization faces this challenge.

THERE ARE TWO TYPES OF VALUES: *ASPIRATIONAL* AND *ACTUAL*. THE FIRST IS WHO YOU WANT TO BE; THE SECOND IS WHO YOU REALLY ARE.

Aspirational values are the values an organization hopes they have. They're idealistic but not realistic. While it may sound harsh, the gap between aspirational values and actual values is an integrity issue.

The word comes from the same root as "integer," which means "whole." To lack integrity is to be fractured or compartmentalized.

People who lack integrity act and behave differently in the different roles or compartments of their lives. You get one version of them in one context and a different version in another. This is duplicitous—it feels fake, deceitful, and untrustworthy.

This is where the breakdown begins. It starts with inconsistency, which leads to a lack of trust, which causes a lack of unity, which eventually threatens the long-term viability of a family, a business, a team, or an organization.

We've all experienced this inconsistency in the values an organization wants to have and the values you actually experience in their culture. It's not just organizations. We recognize this feeling in our relationships—and even in our own lives.

Most people and most organizations don't intend to end up in this place. When they realize it's where they are, most genuinely want to change. Unfortunately, they often don't know how.

Organizational culture is the result of intentional language, behavioral patterns, and expressed values modeled by leadership and implemented at every level of the organization. If there are gaps between aspirational values and actual values, there's a breakdown in your communication and your strategy.

Leaders never outgrow the need to refocus and clarify values. Leaders don't just communicate values; they model them—even when they don't realize that's what they're doing.

Healthy organizations are intentional about who they are and who they're not. But values aren't just something you hang on a wall or build for your website. Because your values are demonstrated every day, they're also challenged.

Every healthy organization asks the tough questions and is open to new information and feedback without becoming insecure or constantly trying to reinvent themselves. These are minor adjustments born out of the desire to become the better, more authentic version of themselves.

Healthy organizations want to get better because they're consumed with the passion and the mission of the organization.

This is why it's critical to evaluate everything you do on the basis of your values and the mission of your organization. In the case of Milestone Church (the organization I lead), we're constantly asking these questions:

- Is this initiative working?
- Are people genuinely experiencing our values?
- Is this helping people know and love Jesus more?
- Are we meeting needs, impacting our city, and developing leaders?

These kinds of questions can be applied to any organization. Be careful—what you learn may be painful to hear, but it's the only way to reveal our gaps and the blind spots we can't see.

"Self-awareness" has become a buzzword in leadership today, but it's incomplete. Without good information you can't make good decisions, but having the information is only one part of the process. You have to be willing to make the necessary changes.

Change is hard for most people, which is a problem because so much of life is seasonal.

Our world is filled with more options than ever before. In response, many organizations try to meet every preference and request—to be everything to everyone. This is incredibly problematic because we create expectations we can't meet. It sets people up for hurt and disappointment.

Programs and initiatives can be a great asset to our organizations because they allow us to specialize, create subcultures, and develop new leaders. But most programs have a shelf life.

Stale programs that have exceeded their expiration date are an energy drain on everybody. They kill momentum and can erode trust in your organization.

This process creates conflict, but it's this kind of healthy conflict that closes the gap between who we are and who we aspire to be.

The same is true in our families and in our personal relationships. When we have enough trust and relational capital to be brutally honest without turning into personal attacks, we gain the opportunity to receive incredibly valuable input and feedback. Without this, we can't have the relationships we really want.

CONFLICT IS THE BRIDGE TO GREATER INTIMACY.

In your closest and most trusted relationships, give people permission to be this honest. At first this makes you feel very vulnerable. Don't worry—you're not alone. We're all a little apprehensive about it. But once you begin to experience the benefit of this in your closest relationships, you'll find the courage to make this a more consistent part of your life.

It's important to remember that when you're the leader, you have to take the initiative. The responsibility comes back to you. You have to be willing to invite this level of honesty. The enemy is your pride, your hubris—the arrogant belief you know better and don't need anyone else's perspective.

It may be hard for you to hear, but it's even harder for them to be honest.

Ask these three simple questions:
- "What would you like me to stop doing?"
- "What would you like me to keep doing?"
- "What would you like me to start doing?"

If the person you're asking trusts you enough to be honest, the chances are good you won't be able to accommodate everything they request. But you will be able to do some of them and you will be aware of the areas in which you need to grow.

And when you keep doing this, eventually you'll close the gap between who you aspire to be and who you are.

Discussion Questions

1. Have you ever been in an organization in which there was a clear gap between their aspirational values and their actual values? How did it impact your ability to do your job?

2. How does the challenge of closing the gap between aspirational values and actual values affect our homes?

3. Are there "programs" at work, in your family, or in your personal life that used to be meaningful but are now stale? Are there better ways to accomplish your values in each of these areas?

Leadership Challenge

— Ask someone on your team at work or in your home one of these questions (it's probably too much to ask all at once):

- "What do you want me to stop doing?"
- "What do you want me to keep doing?"
- "What do you want me to start doing?"

— Listen and write it down. Don't be defensive. Don't argue with them. You don't have to commit in the moment. Take some time and really consider how the suggested change could strengthen your relationship.

27

The Historic Christian Faith

**THOSE WHO DON'T KNOW HISTORY
ARE DOOMED TO REPEAT IT.
— EDMUND BURKE**

In a discussion about winning values, it may seem strange to drop in a chapter about the history of the Christian faith. But if you were leading a company or a sports team, it would be important for you to understand the history of your industry and the different challenges and choices that have brought you to this moment.

With more than 2,000 years of history to summarize in a few pages, I'm obviously not going to give you a deep dive into facts and figures. But I think it's critical for you to have a basic grasp of how we got here. As Mr. Burke famously said, the first step to avoiding the mistakes of our past is to know what they were.

When you gave your life to Christ, you joined a team. You became a part of the body of Christ. The body doesn't exist to advance your agenda. You don't get to decide what the body values.

If you're going to be an effective member of the team, you have to know the values, the strategy, and the game plan of the team. This has always been difficult, but it may be more difficult today than ever before for several cultural reasons.

First, we live in a technology-driven world where the general assumption is that new is good and old is bad. No one is camping out in line for an iPhone 4 or a Palm Pilot. This may be true for our personal devices, but there are many ancient ideas and principles that remain superior to the latest cultural opinions.

Second, our culture is radically individualistic. We say things like, "You do you," or "You be you," which not so subtly implies that the world revolves around us. This is great marketing, but it's completely unbiblical. It also creates deep mistrust for authority, especially in large established structures.

Third, we don't really need to know history because we have Google and Wikipedia. If we ever find ourselves in a situation where we want to know something, we can look it up. Or we can ask Siri or Alexa. This sounds like a good strategy—provided, of course, that the internet is a trustworthy and reliable source. I'll wait for you to finish laughing.

And finally, we view history through an anachronistic filter— meaning, we superimpose *our* cultural norms onto time periods and moments when they did not exist. Biblical norms may appear rigid and old-fashioned today, but in their time they were radically inclusive toward women and children especially.

The combination of these four factors often leads people to think they know better than the Bible and they're free to conveniently pick and choose what parts of the historic Christian faith they're willing to accept while reserving the right to adjust and adapt as they see fit.

I don't recommend this as a helpful strategy. If you want to share in the benefits of following Jesus, you can't pick and choose which parts you're willing to follow.

We're not reinventing or re-creating the wheel. We stand on the shoulders of others who have gone before us and fulfilled the purpose of God in their generation. We have to guard against the constant cultural assumption that we know better than the people of the past.

A brief understanding of the process of how we ended up with what we believe gives us great confidence in our relationship with God.

The technical term for this is "orthodoxy," which simply means "right beliefs." But the Bible makes it clear that it's not enough to *believe* the right things; we also need to *do* the right things. The technical word for this is "orthopraxy"—right practices.

The earliest followers of Jesus picked up His Great Commission to go and make disciples. They started in Jerusalem and have since spread throughout the entire world. The details of this incredible story start in the book of Acts but continue today.

If God is working in you and changing you through this process, it's more than your story—it includes everything that happened beforehand in order to make this possible.

From those earliest days, followers of Christ faced all kinds of difficult decisions in establishing and advancing the mission of the church. The Holy Spirit led them through all kinds of questions, such as whether or not Jesus-followers had to follow the Jewish law (no), how to relate to ungodly authority (obey when possible without violating your conscience), and whether the gospel was only for the Jews or for everyone (the whole world).

But most of the questions back then were similar to the questions we face today: Who is Jesus and how does this change the way we relate to Him?

All of the early controversies centered around Jesus:

- Was Jesus a man? Was Jesus God?
- Did He really have a physical body?
- Did He come to inspire us with spiritual teaching or did He have to die for our sins?
- Did He really die and come back to life with a resurrected body?

The story of the New Testament is the clear consensus the followers of Jesus came to on these matters. It's critical to understand that this was not a series of ideological statements written on scrolls—the apostles all gave their lives for what they believed. Every one of them was martyred because they were unwilling to change their convictions on these central issues (John died of old age in exile after they tried to kill him and he wouldn't die).

This is why John and Peter and Paul all talked about what they'd seen for themselves, what they'd personally experienced, and what they'd received from Jesus that they passed on to us. The history of Christianity is not a group of clever people devising ideological belief systems. It's a supernatural story of ordinary people who personally encountered God.

It may be difficult to imagine why unbelievers would kill these early Christians for their religious beliefs—the reason was that the message of Jesus transformed the lives of people and turned the ancient world on its head. Cultural customs, economies, and established systems of power were overturned as more and more people turned and put their faith in Christ.

The message was not, "Jesus is one way among many to make you feel spiritual; try a little bit to incorporate His positive teachings into your life as you see fit."

The message of the first century was, "Caesar is Lord." This peculiar group of people continued to defiantly insist, "Jesus is LORD."

And more and more people started to listen.

They believed this Good News so strongly that they would rather die than renounce it. This message traveled all around the world; and no matter how hard caesars, kings, emperors, warlords, presidents, or dictators tried to stop it, it continued to grow.

In fact, the more fervently the empires of the world tried to stomp it out, the more it grew.

From Jerusalem, in spite of great persecution, over the next 300 years the message of Jesus spread throughout the entire Roman world. When the Roman empire receded at the hands of the Barbarian tribes (the Goths, the Anglo-Saxons, etc.), the gospel took root in the lives of new believers and their conversion stories began to spread, bringing the message of Jesus to new territory.

This process repeated itself as the Vikings emerged on the world stage. The same ships that carried warriors who pillaged and plundered also brought with them the promise of new life in Christ to distant lands through the lives of genuine disciples who were often servants or even captives.

The message of the gospel finds its way into the story of global expansion through the Middle and Dark Ages, into the era of European colonization, and then finally reaches its greatest global saturation over the last 200 years through the missionary movements based out of the United States.

BECAUSE THE MISSION OF JESUS IS RELATIONAL, IT CAN SPREAD WHEREVER THERE ARE PEOPLE WHO LOVE HIM AND WHO LOVE OTHERS.

This distinction is critical because the means by which the message is carried is not the message. While the gospel traveled along the roads built by the Roman Empire and the long voyages made by Vikings and colonizing Europeans, the gospel is not an endorsement of those cultures.

As has always been the case when you include imperfect people, this expansion and momentum brought with it heresy, hypocrisy, leadership failures, and abuses of power such as the Crusades, the Inquisitions, and the events preceding the Protestant Reformation in the 1500s.

There were many, many more controversies and attempts to sidetrack or alter the message and mission of Jesus—these are only a few of the ones you may have heard about.

But the message of Jesus endured through the power of the Holy Spirit working through His genuine followers. Because Jesus promised to build His Church, no matter how many terrible mistakes are made through frail human leadership, the Church endures according to the mission of Jesus.

As with any organization, churches have unique cultures, values, and personalities. But unlike other organizations, in order to be consistent with the biblical and historic Christian faith, a church must adhere to a set of essentials beliefs.

There's freedom for diversity in the nonessentials, but there must be unity in the essentials.

Most scholars agree, it's difficult to pinpoint the exact date when these essentials were first written down for posterity. But the clear record of several critical councils and subsequent creeds clarifies that the understanding of this orthodoxy was completed and recognized during the AD 300s.

These essentials have been reemphasized and reprioritized over the years, but they have remained fundamentally unchanged. The specific wording varies slightly, but the general consensus is clear.

1. The Bible (and only the Bible) is the authoritative Word of God. It's inspired by the Holy Spirit and remains the final authority in all matters of doctrine.

2. There is one God, eternally existent in three persons: Father, Son, and Holy Spirit.

3. Jesus Christ is the Son of God, the second person of the Trinity—fully God and fully man. He was born of a virgin, lived a perfect sinless life, took the sin of the world onto Himself, and died on the cross to pay the penalty for this sin. He was resurrected to life three days later according to Scripture and ascended into heaven, where He sits at the right hand of the Father, interceding on behalf of the saints.

4. The Holy Spirit, the third person of the Trinity, is the empowering presence of God who always moves in cooperation with God's Word. He convicts the world of sin, lives inside the believer, reminds us of Jesus' words, leads us into truth, gives gifts to His children to serve the church, and continually fills believers with His empowering presence.

5. Salvation comes by grace through faith; we receive the perfect righteousness of Jesus Christ as a gift through His atoning death and resurrection, not as the result of our good works or human effort.

6. The Church is God's body in the earth entrusted with the authority to accomplish the Great Commission. Every person in Christ is a vital part of the family, receives gifts to serve others, and is expected to uphold the unity of the faith.

7. Jesus is coming again at the end of history to judge the world, establish His Kingdom, and inaugurate His eternal reign.

These are the essentials. I hope they sound familiar. This isn't the list for my church; this is the list for Jesus' Church. Without a clear connection to these essentials, you may be spiritual, but you aren't historically Christian.

Remember, because the message is relational, we don't memorize the essentials in order to prepare for taking a test. These are the values by which we live our lives. When we don't understand, we talk about them with each other.

When we don't know what it looks like to live them out, we don't silently and individually wrestle with them until we give up. We turn to our trusted relationships for help and a fresh perspective.

That's exactly what we're going to do. Over the next few chapters, we're going to break down these concepts and consider what it looks like to actually live them out.

After all, this is the way genuine followers of Christ have always done it.

Discussion Questions

1. Name two of the cultural challenges that make it difficult for us to stay faithful to the historic Christian faith. Which one is the most difficult for you?

2. What did most of the early controversies center around? Do you think this is still true today? Why is this so important?

3. Were you familiar with the seven essentials listed? Are they difficult to understand? Is there an essential you don't agree with?

28

Jesus

HE BECAME WHAT WE ARE THAT HE MIGHT MAKE US WHAT HE IS.
— ATHANASIUS OF ALEXANDRIA

Then Jesus asked, "But who do you say I am?"
Matthew 16:15 CEV

In Matthew 16, Jesus asked this question to His disciples, but He asks this same question to every human being who has ever lived: "Who do you say I am?"

It's the most important question any of us will answer. How we respond to Jesus goes a long way in determining the quality and trajectory of our lives. It's the one question we can't afford to miss. And yet, it's a question most people struggle with.

Psalm 118 includes a strange little phrase in verse 22: "The stone the builders rejected has become the cornerstone."

It doesn't seem like a big deal, but verse 23 says it's the Lord who did this and it's marvelous in our eyes. During the last week of His life, Jesus is teaching a group of people and He basically tells them, "God was talking about Me. I'm the cornerstone."[18]

You may have heard one of the well-known songs about Jesus in which He's referred to as the cornerstone, but unless you're a big fan of ancient construction techniques, you probably haven't thought about what it means.

Cornerstones were anchors. They were the first piece set in place for any construction project because they were the foundation everything else was built on. They would often require dozens of men to move using pulleys and levers. If they got this stone wrong, everything would eventually come crashing down.

And the bigger the building project, the larger and more dependable the stone needed to be.

The Bible says Jesus is the cornerstone—of the universe. Colossians 1:16-17 says, "All things have been created through him and for him. He is before all things, and in him all things hold together."

Here's what this means: If you're going to build your life on Jesus, you need to get Him right. If you build your life on a fictional version of Him, then when your foundation is tested, your house will come tumbling down.

As we talked about in chapter 8, "What Does God Want from Me?" this is about our hearts, not a list of doctrinal rules. If we set Jesus as our friend or as a wise moral teacher, it will change the way we relate to Him. When we set Him in our hearts as Lord (see 1 Peter 3:15), it doesn't mean we'll do everything perfectly, but we do predetermine to give Him the final say.

The reason this is so important is that people have so many different opinions of who Jesus is. And in our current cultural landscape, typically the only person considered wrong is the one brazen enough to believe they're right.

When it comes to Jesus, not every answer is equal. All opinions are not valid. He knew this. It's the reason He quoted the song from Psalm 118. Most people had no idea who He was or what He was doing. And most people—especially those who were threatened by Him—refused to take Him at His word.

PEOPLE HAVE ALWAYS LIKED TO INTERPRET JESUS ON THE BASIS OF WHO THEY WANT HIM TO BE. HOWEVER, JESUS IS NOT A HYPOCRITE. HE CAN'T BE LESS THAN WHO HE IS.

Passionate, well-intended people have greatly misidentified Him from the time He was born, throughout His life, and in every age since. During this same span, deceitful and manipulative people have attempted to alter or discredit His identity.

All of the early controversies and heresies (wrong teachings) were perversions of the identity and significance of Jesus. If you get Jesus wrong, eventually you get everything wrong. That's what makes Him the cornerstone.

And yet, the genuine Jesus endures—not as a symbol; not as an idea, a figurehead, or a religious institution—but as an authentic, living person willing to welcome all who would receive Him.

By any metric, Jesus of Nazareth is the most influential human being who ever lived. He never got married, never had kids, never sat on an earthly throne, never constructed a palace, and never started a Fortune 500 company. Yet, 2,000 years later, more than two billion people worship Him. More books, paintings, songs, schools, hospitals, and organizations have been created in His name than any person who's ever lived.

I believe He's earned the courtesy any of us would desire—the ability to speak for Himself.

Here's what the Bible says about Jesus:

1. He's fully God.

He was more than a rabbi, more than a great teacher, more than a prophet, more than even a king. Somehow the idea that Jesus never claimed to be God continues to linger—but certainly not among anyone with a basic understanding of first-century Judaism. More than performing miracles, Jesus received worship, forgave sin, claimed to be the subject of all of Scripture, and equated Himself with God—even to the point of referring to Himself with God's most sacred name.

2. He's fully man.

Scholars call this the incarnation, and it's one of the most mind-blowing things about Jesus. It's hard for us to wrap our minds around it. How does an infinite God become a baby? Yet, the Bible won't back down from this idea. One of the oldest portions of the entire New Testament, Philippians 2:6-7, tells us that Jesus didn't see equality with God as something to be used for His advantage. He took on the form of a servant and humbled Himself by becoming a man.

One of the earliest challenges to the church claimed that Jesus didn't have a physical body because the physical is evil and the spiritual world is light and immaterial. John challenges this misguided view. John stakes one whole letter (1 John) on the idea that they heard Him with their ears, saw Him with their eyes, and touched Him—the Son who was with the Father and came to be with us.

3. He's the King of the universe.

The same passage in Philippians 2 continues to say that because He humbled Himself, God exalted Him and gave Him the name above every other name, and that at the name of Jesus every knee would bow and tongue confess that Jesus is Lord to the glory of the Father.

Every emperor, every king, every dictator, every president, every self-important celebrity, every self-sufficient CEO, every atheist, every critic, and every man, woman, and child—we're all going to bow and recognize His eternal reign.

Not just every knee on Earth, but in heaven, and under the earth. In other words, throughout the entire universe. Daniel 7 talks about this King whose dominion is everlasting and whose Kingdom can never be destroyed.

Sometimes people ask, "What about aliens?" It's an interesting question. The Bible doesn't go into specifics, but it's clear: If there's any life out there beyond the earth, Jesus is Lord over them, too.

4. He lived a sinless life.

He lived the life we should have lived but could not. Where all of humankind went wrong in the Garden with Adam, He came and restored the way through living a perfect life. He didn't just do this as an example; He did it in our place so that His righteous record could be given to us.

He was tempted in every way. He experienced every form of suffering, betrayal, injustice, and abuse. He took all of our pain onto Himself, not because He was guilty, but because He was willing.

The title Jesus used to describe Himself, "the Son of Man," also comes from Daniel 7, and it means "the true son" or "the perfect human." Another similar term used later was "the second Adam"—the one worthy of being re-entrusted with the stewardship of God's good Creation.

5. He was born of a virgin.

Our world is radically individualistic. We believe we're the captains of our own fate and that we stand on our own merit. The problem is, we all carry traits and flaws passed down through our family line. It can be traced all the way back to Adam. We don't become sinners once we sin; we sin because we're sinners. Our flaws and brokenness come hard-wired from the factory.

Because Jesus was conceived by the Holy Spirit, He didn't carry the sin line passed down from Adam. Because He was not born into sin, He had the opportunity to make right what had gone wrong for all humanity as the second (and faithful) Adam.

6. He died in our place.

Sin—the failure to uphold the righteous standard of God—separates us from a perfect God. Sin always leads to death, both in its own natural outcome and in the punishment it requires.

Even though He was the only person to ever live a righteous life, Jesus took the sin of the world upon Himself and paid the penalty for the sin of mankind through His atoning death.

Crucifixion was a humiliating way to die. In the Roman custom, the person was hung from a cross on a well-traveled road and died of asphyxiation. The reason for this was to inspire fear and obedience from the passersby who would hear the last words of the dying man.

Jesus' last words, "It is finished," were a declaration of the payment, the ransom He offered to satisfy the chasm between sinful man and a righteous God. The Lamb of God became the Passover Lamb for the universe. Nothing more needed to be added.

This is why the massive veil separating the Holy of Holies in the temple ripped. The barrier separating God's presence from sinful mankind had been torn down through the ultimate sacrifice of the perfect Lamb of God.

For the record, Jesus was fully dead. He wasn't asleep. He wasn't kidnapped. He wasn't in a coma. He was *dead* dead.

7. He was physically resurrected to a glorified body.

The chief priests and Pharisees knew that Jesus had promised to rise again on the third day, so they went to Pilate and asked him to prevent this from happening. The Roman governor instructed his soldiers to make it as secure as they could, so they placed a seal on the tomb and sent guards to watch over it.

On Sunday morning, there was a violent earthquake, an angel moved the stone, and the resurrected Jesus walked out. He was dead, but He didn't stay dead. Death no longer had power over Him.

When He met with His friends and followers, they were overwhelmed; they were afraid; they were ecstatic—and just to eliminate any doubt, Jesus invited them to touch Him. He wasn't a ghost. He met Peter, James, John, and Andrew on the same shore where He first called them and ate breakfast.

The Church was built on the preaching of the cross and the resurrection—historical factual events, not abstract spiritual ideas.

When people started to claim that this didn't happen or that it was only a beautiful metaphor, the apostle Paul wasn't having it. He said that if the resurrection didn't happen, then Christianity was a waste of time, all of humanity was still in their sin, all faith is futile, and followers of Christ should be pitied more than any other group on the planet.[19]

He didn't leave any gray area.

8. He's coming back again.

Jesus used parables to preach, and one of the most common setups was the idea of a king who went away and came back. He talked at length about coming back to judge the world. He would separate wheat from chaff or weeds. He would separate sheep from goats. He would separate those who built on the rock from those who built on the sand. He would come back for a wedding feast. He would come back to check on His workers, and on and on and on.

The way we pass this judgment is not through accumulating enough spiritual deeds while avoiding bad choices. Our hope is in a genuine, trusting relationship with Jesus.

He also said that no one knows the date or the hour. So don't waste time predicting or speculating on when this might happen, but instead, keep doing what He told us to do until He returns.

JESUS STANDS ALONE. THERE'S NO ONE LIKE HIM.

This is why there's no other way to have peace with God outside of Jesus. If we don't get Jesus right, eventually everything else will go wrong.

This Jesus demands a response. He invites everyone to come to Him. He receives us as we are and then begins to change us into the person He created us to be. This can be your moment.

Romans 10:9-10 says, "If you declare with your mouth, 'Jesus is Lord,' and believe in your heart that God raised Him from the dead, you will be saved. For it is with your heart that you believe and are justified, and it is with your mouth that you profess your faith and are saved."

If you're ready, let's pray this simple prayer together: "Jesus, I believe You are who You say You are. I believe You died for my sins. I believe God raised You from the dead. I put my trust in You. I receive Your perfect righteousness and I give You my life."

Congratulations! If you prayed this prayer, the Bible says that all of heaven is rejoicing because you've come home. You're a new creation in Christ. And like a newborn baby, you're going to need some help!

Here's what you should do now:
- Tell your group.
- If you're not in a group, tell someone at your church.
- If you've never been water baptized, go back and read chapter 7 and make that your next step!

Discussion Questions

1. Why is Jesus called the cornerstone? What would it mean if Jesus was the cornerstone of your life?

2. How do we know Jesus claimed to be God?

3. Why did Jesus have to die? What does it mean to say, "He died in our place"?

4. Does it matter if you believe Jesus physically rose from the dead? Why? What did the apostle Paul think about it?

Leadership Challenge

— Test yourself to see how many of the eight characteristics of Jesus you can remember without looking. Practice it until you can consistently recall all of them.

29

The Bible

**A THOROUGH KNOWLEDGE OF THE BIBLE IS WORTH MORE
THAN A COLLEGE EDUCATION.
— THEODORE ROOSEVELT**

*So faith comes from hearing, and hearing through
the word of Christ.*
Romans 10:17 ESV

The Christian faith always begins and ends with Jesus—the living Word. But we also have been entrusted with the incredible gift of God's Word. The Bible is central. The Bible is timeless.

And the Bible is the primary means by which we understand God's nature. It's how we learn to hear His voice, and it's how we understand how He's created us to live.

Studies show that the majority of people would like to know more about the Bible. When I've asked people what they want me to preach on, one of the most common responses is, "I want to learn more about the Bible."

This is good news.

The problem is, for most people, this is much more of an aspirational value than an actual one. In my experience, there are far more people *around* the Bible than those who are *in* their Bible.

Access is not our problem. Most of us don't realize that for the majority of Christian history, very few believers owned a copy of Scripture or had the ability to read. It's hard for us to understand how fortunate we are.

We have e-bibles, audio Bibles, Bible apps, and Bibles of every translation with every kind of cool packaging—but we have fewer people actually reading and understanding the Bible.

However, this challenge can be corrected. I've seen it happen over and over. With a little intentionality and commitment, I believe anyone can grow in this area if they make it a priority.

Reading a book like this gives you a huge boost in the process.

If you've been taking the time to look up the scriptures and answer the questions as you've been working your way through this book, and if you've been talking about it with others, then you already know and understand the Bible more than you did when you started.

This is how it works.

When you set out to read the Bible, two problems quickly emerge: *I don't have time, and I don't understand.*

The time issue is pretty simple. You make time for what you care about.

IF READING THE BIBLE IS IMPORTANT, YOU'LL FIND A WAY TO GET IT DONE.

There are all kinds of helpful habit-forming tips to guide us in the process. It's never been easier to track our personal data than it is today—10,000 steps, 8 glasses of water/day, 30 minutes of exercise, 8 hours of sleep.

Routines, consistency, and location all create powerful habits. Experts tell us that creating designated spaces for certain activities creates triggers that reinforce healthy patterns of behavior: *the bed is for sleeping; drink a glass of water first thing each morning when you walk in the kitchen; pick the same chair for reading.*

Immediate and drastic lifestyle changes based on gimmicks are very difficult to sustain. However, consistent attainable repetition creates muscle memory and long-term change.

This is why it's a better approach to read the Bible even 5 minutes every day than to read it once a week for an hour at a time. And once you hit 5 minutes, you can grow to 10, 15, 20, 30—and before long an hour seems possible.

This is also why I recommend that new Bible readers avoid electronic devices as their primary Bible because the nonstop notifications are both incredibly distracting and capable of taking up all your time. You have to train your mind and attention to stay focused.

This is more difficult for us than any previous generation, but it can be done.

The other big problem new Bible readers face is the struggle to understand what they're reading. While there's certainly a learning curve, one of the greatest attributes of the Bible is that it's simple enough to capture the imagination of a child and profound enough to puzzle the deepest thinker.

Understanding the Bible always comes back to context: *Who's writing the book? Who were they writing to? What was happening in their world at the time? What style/genre of writing is it (historical narrative, wisdom [proverbs/psalms/poetry], prophecy, gospel, apocalyptic, etc.)?* Context gives you the best opportunity to get the intended meaning.

Remember, the Bible is a library of 66 books written by more than 40 authors over a period of 1,500 years to tell one big story. Every book, chapter, and verse points us to the person of Jesus. This process was inspired and superintended by the Holy Spirit—not for the purpose of delivering religious rules or providing spiritual information. Rather, the primary purpose of the Bible is to show us the nature and character of God.

The Bible was written thousands of years ago, halfway around the world, in languages we don't speak, and yet the words have the power to jump off the page and judge every thought and intention of our hearts—right now in this moment.

You might think, *How do I know if I'm winning with my Bible?* That's a great question. I believe there are two clear signs this is happening.

First, your time in the Word is changing you. It builds your character by challenging your mindsets and changing your perspective. You're filled with new wonder and appreciation for the goodness of God. You're more aware of your selfishness and your tendency toward idolatry.

Serving idols doesn't mean you bow down to the kind of statues you might find in a museum; it means you take a good thing and make it the most important thing in your life. The Bible helps us identify this pattern in our hearts because this tendency lurks in every human being. The Word turns our heart and attention back to Jesus.

Second, you're consistently filled with faith. Romans 10:17 tells us that the way we grow in faith is hearing the Word. This is why it's important to read the Bible out loud, to memorize it, to put it in places where you'll see it every day, like the back of your phone, your bathroom mirror, or the dash of your car. Faith causes us to trust God's promises no matter what we're facing.

The sweet spot in Bible reading is gaining the confidence to know you can start today and benefit from what you're reading, while maintaining a humble posture ready to understand God's Word through trusted voices.

How Do I Get Started?

1. Study the Word in church.
Listen, pay attention, take notes, reflect on it during the week, and talk about it with your friends/family/small group. You'll learn how to do this on your own as you do it with your church family.

2. Commit to read every day.
Pick a time frame you can consistently hit, even if it's 5-10 minutes. As it becomes a habit, increase the number.

3. Start in the Gospel of John (fourth book of the New Testament).
John explains the significance of what's happening during Jesus' life, so it's the best place to start. If you have time, read one psalm (how we relate to God) and one proverb (how we relate to each other) each day. Once you finish John, read Luke and Acts—it's one big story describing Jesus' life and ministry through the foundation and early adventures of the Church.

4. Use the S.O.A.P. method.
You start with **S**cripture, you **O**bserve what's happening in the original context, you **A**pply it to your life, and then you **P**ray. This will greatly help your understanding.

5. Confess God's Word.
This means to pray or read out loud a passage of Scripture every day. When you do this, you'll get used to hearing the Word come out of your mouth and your heart will align with God's.

Discussion Questions

1. What makes reading the Bible difficult? What practical steps are you taking to overcome this challenge?

2. What is the primary purpose of the Bible? How does that impact the way we read it?

3. What are some practical things you can do to become more consistent in your Bible reading?

Leadership Challenge

— Memorize a verse of Scripture this week and be prepared to recite it to someone. To help you, put the verse where you can see it (the dash of your car, your bathroom mirror, the back of your phone etc.).

— See if you can build a streak of reading your Bible for five days. Then go for ten. Challenge yourself to continue to set a personal best on a regular basis.

30

The Holy Spirit

But I tell you the truth, it is to your advantage that I go away; for if I do not go away, the Helper will not come to you; but if I go, I will send Him to you. – Jesus
John 16:7 NASB

Jesus loves His Church and He also loves the Helper, the Advocate—
the Holy Spirit.

He's the least-discussed member of the Trinity. Most people understand God the Father and Jesus—but we're not sure what we're supposed to do with the other guy.

Jesus said that when He left to be with His Father, it would be to our advantage because He would send the Spirit to us. This made no sense to the disciples. They could not imagine life without Jesus. The idea that it would actually be better would have blown their minds.

This is often how people feel about the Holy Spirit. They don't have a category to put Him in. The Spirit is not weird, although sometimes the way people respond to Him may be.

THE HOLY SPIRIT IS A PERSON—NOT A MIST, A VAPOR, OR A FEELING.

The Holy Spirit is not a style of church or worship service. There was a time when people thought a church was edgy if they didn't have pews, if they had a band instead of an organ, and if people raised their hands during worship. Some of this depends on your upbringing and your expectations.

The Holy Spirit is not a license to be spontaneous, hyper-emotional, and overly spiritual. Often in church well-meaning people can unknowingly make things weird. The Holy Spirit doesn't always make us comfortable, but He's also not into strange for the sake of strange.

In John 14, Jesus said it's the Holy Spirit who leads us and guides us into truth and reminds us of what Jesus has said. In John 15, Jesus said the Spirit testifies about Him and empowers us to do the same. In John 16, Jesus said the Holy Spirit convicts the world of sin and judgment.

And before Jesus ascends into heaven to be with His Father, He tells His disciples to wait in the city for the promise from the Father, the gift of the Holy Spirit, which would give them power.

This power comes in the upper room in Acts 2 and leads to the preaching of the first sermon and to thousands of people repenting and giving their lives to Christ.

Because of this passage (and others throughout the New Testament), when I hear a phrase like "The Holy Spirit is really moving at that church," my first thought is not some deep obscure teaching or unusual expression of worship but crowds of people who were far from God repenting and discovering new life in Christ.

Some people read this and believe it was a one-time deal that Jesus used to get the party started. This perspective may be convincing—until you read the rest of the encounters in the book of Acts.

People will often ask, "Do you have to believe the Spirit is continually present and available and working in our lives to be a follower of Christ?" I understand that devout followers can wrestle with this question because they're apprehensive about the subject. In the church I grew up in, we weren't necessarily against the Holy Spirit, but we never really talked about Him.

There's a range of perspectives that don't rise to the level of the theological essentials we listed in chapter 27. Nearly all of the statements regarding the Holy Spirit are agreed upon between all the parties in this discussion.

For the most part, there are two big points of contention. **The first fork in the road is whether or not there is a subsequent work of the Holy Spirit.** The Bible is clear that when a person gives their life to Christ, the Holy Spirit comes and lives inside of them. This is not disputed. Some people believe that if you make a big point about a subsequent work of the Holy Spirit, you diminish the power of salvation. This leads them to dismiss the need for a subsequent work.

A clear understanding of justification and sanctification becomes very helpful. When we repent of our sin and put our faith in Jesus, we are born again. We receive a new nature and are credited with the perfect righteousness of Jesus in our relationship with God. We can't earn this and nothing can be added to it. This is justification—this gift is a one-time moment.

This gift includes the empowering presence of the Holy Spirit, which helps in the process of becoming the person God created us to be. This process is called sanctification. In 2 Corinthians 1:22, Paul tells us that God puts His Spirit in our hearts as a deposit of what's to come. In this way, the Spirit is the sign that He has received us in His family and the promise that He's going to continue to work in us. And one of the primary vehicles of this ongoing work is the Holy Spirit.

For example, if we look at the life of Peter, in John 20, he encounters the resurrected Jesus and receives the Holy Spirit. Jesus tells the disciples to wait in the city until they receive the power of the promise. This happens in Acts 2 in the upper room on the day of Pentecost. They're filled with the Spirit, and by the end of the chapter, Peter preaches his first message with boldness and power and thousands of people repent.

In Acts 4, Peter is filled with the Spirit and begins to speak again, this time to a group of religious leaders who are trying to keep him from preaching about Jesus. He speaks so boldly that they don't know what to do with him. Eventually they let him go and he heads over to a prayer meeting. They're praying and celebrating and the room begins to shake and the Bible says they were all filled with the Spirit and spoke the Word of God boldly.

Peter is not the same. He has a new nature and new boldness. He's preaching and bearing fruit, and yet he's continually being filled with the Spirit. Some people may say this was a one-time deal God did for the apostles, but later in his letter to the Ephesians, Paul encourages everyone to be continuously filled with the Spirit.

In Ephesians 5:18, he writes, "Do not get drunk on wine, which leads to debauchery. Instead, be filled with the Spirit." Ephesians 5 is all about how to imitate God and live a holy life. The following passage is the section we looked at where Paul challenges husbands to love their wives like Jesus loves the church.

The Greek word for "filled" is the verb *pleroo*, and it means "to abound," "to be completely filled," "to overflow." Here are several key concepts about this word. First, it's an imperative command. It's not a suggestion. Second, it's plural, so it means it's for everyone. Third, it's passive, so it's not something you do to yourself; you're acted on by an outside force. And finally, it's in the present tense, so it's not something that happened in the past but is ongoing and continually available.

The concept is a repetitive filling. This is why he contrasts being drunk with wine—when you need comfort, when you're celebrating, don't get drunk. That creates problems. Instead, be filled with the Spirit.

The problem is often with semantics. People get tripped up over words/phrases like "baptism of the Spirit," "filled," "overflowing," or "ongoing." It's less about labels and categories and more about a general openness to God working in your life through the Holy Spirit. It's a willingness to receive the power and the presence of the Holy Spirit that points people to God as you love and serve them.

The second sticking point is whether or not God still works through the gifts of the Spirit and performs miracles.

Is God still moving in power, or was that expression reserved for the early church?

All churches believe that God gave gifts (Greek word *charis*) to the apostles to build the church. Some churches believed this was a temporary approach until the Bible was completed, at which point the gifts stopped, or ceased.

The rationale comes from 1 Corinthians 13:8-10, where a variety of spiritual gifts are listed followed by this phrase: "when the perfect comes, the partial will pass away" (ESV). This group reads "the perfect" as the Bible. While I certainly believe the Bible is perfect, I don't believe this is what this verse is referring to. Verse 12 says that when this same perfect comes, we'll know fully, even as we're fully known.

I respectfully disagree with this line of thinking because, as amazing as the Bible is, I can't say I know Jesus as fully as He knows me.

Other churches believe God gave these gifts to all believers and they continue to be in use for the common good of the people and the mission of the church. They also believe in the continuing, empowering work of the Holy Spirit from the first point.

If you grew up in a spiritual environment with strong opinions on this subject, moving forward with clarity can be difficult. It's easy to feel like we're disrespecting the desires of our family or undermining the validity of our spiritual heritage. This is not theory to me.

I'm grateful for my heritage and all of the development I received. God used it. But I had to admit that my perspective on this subject was based on my limited understanding and my perceptions of abuse in other church environments. I never really took the time to research what the Bible said.

After extensive study on the subject, I came to the conclusion these concepts were always there. I missed them because my conclusions were rooted in my tradition and my Western viewpoint, not what lined up with Scripture.

It was not my experience that drove these changes—it was the Bible.

Since that time, I've benefited from and experienced the power that comes from the ongoing work of the Spirit. I've seen Him move through healing, the healthy expression of the gifts of the Spirit, increased boldness, and His empowering presence.

My goal is not to settle the discussion for you but to give you enough context to come to a conviction on your own. It's worth your time and effort to clarify what you believe on this issue while being gracious and respectful to those who see it differently.

Pragmatic people can disagree, but I think it's easy to overlook the reality that what you believe about this impacts the culture of your environments—your home, your business, and certainly your church. Places where people believe God is present in His Spirit—to encourage, to empower, to lead and guide into truth, and to remind us of what Jesus said—are different.

HERE'S THE BOTTOM LINE: THE PURPOSE OF ON-GOING ENCOUNTERS WITH THE HOLY SPIRIT IS TO PROVIDE POWER FOR A PURPOSE.

It's not emotionalism or more expressive worship services. Those things may happen, but they're not the goal. Remember what happened with Peter—he spoke with boldness.

In Acts 1:8 Jesus told His disciples, "But you will receive power when the Holy Spirit comes on you; and you will be my witnesses in Jerusalem, and in all Judea and Samaria, and to the ends of the earth." This promise provides the power to live the Great Commission—the last words Jesus spoke to His disciples and His clear will for every one of His followers to participate in.

If Jesus spent three years training, teaching, coaching, and correcting these guys personally, and He still believed they would need this kind of power, then we probably need it too.

Discussion Questions

1. What are two things that Jesus said the Holy Spirit would do?

2. What's the primary difference between a Cessationist and a Continuationist? Is this a Christian essential? Can we respectfully disagree?

3. What is the purpose of ongoing encounters with the Holy Spirit? Have you had one of these moments?

31

The Church

*And I tell you that you are Peter, and on this rock
I will build my church, and the gates of Hades will not
overcome it. – Jesus*
Matthew 16:18

If we're following Jesus and building according to His pattern, we have to value what He values. This may seem obvious, but Jesus is really into His Church.

Now I'm self-aware enough to realize this sounds incredibly self-serving. Don't forget where we started: I want more for you than I want from you.

We're used to being sold. Today when we go to the store to get food, some clothes, or a TV, they all want our contact information. Most of us know why—they want our data so they can sell us more stuff.

This is not what the church is about. You don't get a membership card for convenience and then throw it in a stack.

When the Bible talks about becoming a part of a church, it uses the language of family, not a volunteer group or social club.

Most guys have a hard time seeing this, but being planted and engaged in a local church gives you a massive advantage in life. It will help you win every day, not just in spiritual matters, but in every area of your life.

The typical busy dad understands that it's good for his kids to be around church and that his wife will probably be happy with him for going, but he's trying to get through the service. It's not the highlight of his week.

I believe two of the biggest barriers men have with the church are (1) they can't see the benefit beyond getting some extra credit spiritually, and (2) they're not expecting to make meaningful relationships with other men.

The irony is, these are the areas in which the church can have the biggest impact on men—giving them the ability to win at work, at home, in their character, and with their kids. And the best place to find strong, gifted men with godly character is the local church.

It's tragic when men cut themselves off from the very source capable of meeting their deepest needs.

JESUS PROMISED TO BUILD HIS CHURCH.

He knows it has problems. He knows its reputation has suffered. He knows it's not perfect. Yet, He's really into it.

Jesus referenced the gates of Hades not overcoming the Church because it was a real place—it was the cave He was standing next to when He made this statement. He chose this location to talk to His disciples about His Church. Local people believed the ground opened up to the underworld. All sorts of demonic ceremonies were conducted there. A devout person wouldn't even go near this location, but Jesus went there to show them that His Church would work even in the darkest places of our world.

Ephesians 5 tells us Jesus sees the Church as the love of His life. He serves and leads it like His bride.

Granted, this can get uncomfortable quickly, but it can also be really helpful.

I'm sure you've heard some version of one of these statements: "I like Jesus but the church is filled with hypocrites," or "Jesus and I have an understanding and we don't need anybody else." The average person thinks this makes sense because they've met at least one religious hypocrite, and they may have had a bad experience with church.

If we made decisions based only on our experiences, then this seems like a wise choice.

However, if Jesus really views the Church as His wife, then this is like saying, "Jesus, I like You, but Your wife is a disaster," or "You're a great friend. Let's get together, but don't ever bring Your wife."

You won't find this approach in *How to Win Friends and Influence People.*[20]

If you're constantly bad-mouthing and criticizing someone in front of the person who loves them the most, it's not going to help your relationship.

Does the church need to mature and grow? Without a doubt. Are there hypocrites in every church? Definitely.

Of course, there are also hypocrites in every workplace, every classroom, every family, every workout facility, every hobby group—everywhere there are people. As we've already discussed, every one of us has gaps between the person we aspire to be and the person we actually are. This is how life works.

If a restaurant messes up your order, you don't stop eating food.
If a teacher lies, you don't give up on learning.

If an accountant cheats, you don't quit budgeting your money.
If a doctor falsely diagnoses your sickness, you don't walk away from medicine or treatment.

Yet, for some reason, when people have a negative interaction with church, they often give up on the church—and even God.

All these things are valuable, but church is the one place Jesus said, "I'm responsible for making sure we get this right." This is why, no matter how badly people mess up the church—though global political superpowers and Fortune 500 companies come and go—the church keeps trucking along.

The church is a family; it's a body, but it's also an incredible leadership environment. It's easy to miss this.

There was a time as a young man when I looked at the church as a leadership void. It was hard to find the kind of strategic, passionate leadership capable of capturing the imagination and calling of driven men. This has changed.

Renowned leadership experts like Jim Collins, Simon Sinek, Malcolm Gladwell, and Seth Godin have been surprised to find some of their most committed audiences among church leaders and pastors. And all of these gifted men have said they've benefited from the interactions and value they've received through working with churches that are serious about leading people and changing culture.

Ephesians 3:10 says the manifold wisdom of God is made known to the rulers and authorities in the heavenly realms through the church. "Manifold" means "multifaceted"—it's like the entire color spectrum.

God doesn't speak to one kind of person; He speaks to everyone. And the way even His enemies hear His Word is when His Church comes together on His behalf. God's plan for His Church is more than a rescue center from a cruel and dark world; it's mission command for His cosmic takeover.

When it's healthy, the local church is the most resource rich environment on the planet. It's the place where people from every background, every generation, every cultural and ethnic heritage, every diverse skill and ability, come together to form a family.

WE LIKE TO SAY, "WE'RE AN EVERYONE CHURCH."

What we mean is that every person has a part to play. Every person's contribution makes a difference. Ephesians 4:16 describes the church as a body that grows and builds itself up in love as each part adds their effort and ability. What a powerful idea.

As the church grows, it becomes more loving, more dynamic, more expressive in its diverse capacity to demonstrate the love of God.

You may be able to dismiss one talented speaker or a gifted singer as an anomaly. But it's difficult to explain away a group of guys standing in the freezing rain who lead you to the front door where a couple warmly greets you and walks you over to your kids' check-in.

Along the way you meet several different people who smile and offer to help you. When you find your seat, you recognize a couple from school and a family from one of your kids' sports teams. They both tell you how happy they are to see you.

When you're surrounded by this kind of encouragement and support, you experience the worship service differently. You start to think, *There must be something to this.*

By the time you sit down and listen to the message, something inside of you helps you realize this is all more than a coincidence.

Something supernatural is happening. It's more than a group of like-minded people wanting to welcome you to a group. God is speaking. He's telling you how much He loves you. He's drawing you into a genuine relationship.

As you're reflecting on what just happened and how different it was from what you expected, even the most reluctant husband ends up telling his wife, "Unfortunately, I liked it."

It's more than a building, a program, or an event. When God's people gather together in His name to welcome others, this environment becomes the most naturally evangelistic setting in the world.

In an everyone church, behind these friendly, engaged, generous people is a loving Father always working to welcome new people into His family.

Jesus only promised to build *one* thing—His Church. The Church is plan A and there is no plan B. The Church is His body, His hands and feet working in the earth. He distributes His resources—everything we need for life and godliness—through His spiritual family, the Church.

Now, hopefully by chapter 31 you've realized that Jesus cares about you, your career, your marriage, your kids, and even your hobbies and friendships. But those things aren't His driving motivation. We receive the best version of these things as we continue to live in right relationship with Jesus and His Church.

Don't hear what I'm not saying. I'm not pitting your church life against the rest of your life. I don't expect anyone to live at the church.

I think you can be very engaged with your business, your family, your kids' extracurricular activities, and your hobbies and still be engaged with your church.

I think your kids can get good grades, be active in sports, serve as class president, and be engaged in church.

As someone who spent years juggling complex teen schedules filled with every kind of extracurricular activity, I know that the deposits my children received in church now carry them in adulthood. I may be a pastor, but all my children have benefited greatly from small-group leaders, volunteers, student pastors, and a host of other environments they could only experience in the local church.

Each of us has time and responsibility limits, but I've always found we're far more productive and fulfilled when we're intentional with our time and priorities.

What I'm really after is a perspective shift. The details aren't the problem. If you view church as a mildly beneficial option you attend when you have a free weekend, then you won't ever come close to receiving what God created you for.

This shift moves you from a casual observer to a contributor. You stop thinking about you. While it's not natural for us to think this way, here's what I know for certain: If you bring a friend or a family member to church who doesn't have a relationship with Jesus, you are hoping every person in the church is thinking, *I'm here because I love Jesus and there's nothing more important than when someone gives their life to Him.*

It may seem small, but when you make this shift you put yourself in a position to experience the power and presence of Jesus in a different way. Not only will you enjoy it more, but it also creates a desire to grow in all kinds of ways.

- You develop character as you walk with mature believers.
- You learn humility from trusted relationships.
- You receive wisdom from people who are gifted in ways you're not.
- You discover opportunities to serve, which makes you more generous.
- You become a more effective leader at home and in your workplace.

We haven't even discussed how it impacts the rest of your family; we've only looked at what it does for you. But the starting place for real growth is "How can I serve someone else?" instead of "What do I get out of this?"

This is what makes a spiritual family healthy—it also works in our natural families. When each member of the family puts their needs and desires above everyone else, no one ends up happy or fulfilled. It always ends in unmet expectations, hurt feelings, and broken relationships.

But when a family rallies around a common goal with each person contributing their gifts with a loving attitude, an ordinary home project can be as fulfilling as an elaborate vacation.

Discussion Questions

1. What are the two biggest problems most men have with church? Have you wrestled with these?

2. How does Jesus feel about His Church?

3. What is "spiritual family"? What does a healthy spiritual family do?

Leadership Challenge

— Ask God to help you go from "What am I getting out of this?" to "Help me to add value to someone else. Help me to contribute to what You're doing."

32

Spiritual Family

But to all who did receive him, who believed in his name,
he gave the right to become children of God.
John 1:12 ESV

See what great love the Father has lavished on us, that we
should be called children of God! And that is what we are!
1 John 3:1a NIV

For this reason I bow my knees before the Father, from
whom every family in heaven and on earth derives its name.
Ephesians 3:14-15 NASB

Once you realize Jesus really cares about His Church, He views it as His bride, it's the one thing He promised to build, it's His spiritual family, and it's a great place for leadership development, then you still have to figure out how you're actually going to do it.

Like every other organization in the world, a church has values; it has a strategy (even if it's not clearly defined); it has a unique culture.

There are lots of ways to do church.

You can build a convention center where large numbers of people come and watch the services. There are a lot of places doing this well. The services are engaging, they're highly produced, they attract big followings, and the audience primarily participates by watching and being inspired by very gifted people on the platform.

You can do church through a network of smaller programs and classes. The people primarily engage through participating in teaching-based learning settings with planned curriculum punctuated by off-site retreats or gatherings.

You can join a traditional model featuring ceremonial services like the Catholic Mass or mainline liturgy and sacraments.

You can go cause-driven where the church is known for their involvement in a particular mission to address a societal need.

All of these options are prominent and readily available today.

We choose to do church like a family. I try to lead the church like a dad. This may sound a little strange, but as we've seen, this isn't my idea—it's what the Bible says. God intended the church to function like a family.

We believe a church isn't a group of people who gather together to listen to spiritual content. It's God's family in the earth. What does it mean to be engaged in His Church? You don't just watch a podcast and listen to worship music in your car. You attend, you serve, you give, you lead, you get your family in church, you support your pastor, and you value what Jesus values.

Not everyone is comfortable with this approach, and I understand. There's plenty of room for different expressions. But I believe this is the way God wants us to build.

I try to care for people the way I would care for my family, and this is how we want our staff, our volunteers, and even our guests to relate to each other. This model is not for everyone, but it's the one most widely depicted in Scripture and produces extraordinary results.

Nothing is more fulfilling to me than to help someone else take steps in their relationship with God.

I'm convinced the best way to help people grow spiritually and be developed is in the context of genuine, committed relationships that grow out of spiritual family.

Some people are looking for this. Others have given up hope they'll ever find it. Still others can't articulate that this is what they've been wanting until they experience it.

What Keeps People from Spiritual Family?

1. They can't see it.
Jesus said His Kingdom was like a treasure buried in a field. It's easy to miss. You could walk past it without realizing it's there. But once you discover it, you'll do whatever it takes to get it.

I understand that the concept of spiritual family is not widely known, but like the treasure in Jesus' story, it's always been there. The early church knew how valuable it was. John starts his Gospel by highlighting this amazing opportunity: "But to all who did receive him, who believed in his name, he gave the right to become children of God" (John 1:12, ESV). In other words, anyone who received God and believed in Jesus was given the incredible privilege of being welcomed into God's family.

Years later, when he's writing a letter to a group of believers, he hasn't lost any of the awe and wonder that God would call us His children. He needs two exclamation points to communicate the depth of his emotion: "See what great love the Father has lavished on us, that we should be called children of God! And that is what we are!" (1 John 3:1a).

Paul reminded the church in Ephesus that God is so involved in our lives, He gives every single family on the planet their name, their identity, and their unique distinctive. He has a vision and a plan for every family. "For this reason I bow my knees before the Father, from whom every family in heaven and on earth derives its name" (Ephesians 3:14-15, NASB).

2. They've had painful experiences with family.

I realize spiritual family can sound overly idealistic and naïve. I've worked with people long enough to know how much pain there is in this area of our lives. No one else can love us like our family, and no one else can hurt us as intensely either.

If your pain is deep enough, just the mention of the phrase "spiritual family" makes you uncomfortable because it implies God was behind it.

I get it. I really do.

However, God's vision for your family is always meant to bless you, to encourage you, to inspire you, to give you the power to create a home and a culture in which everyone freely gives and receives love, forgives quickly, and serves one another with generous, unconditional love. He wants this for your family because it's the culture of His family.

3. Spiritual family is countercultural.

Spiritual family may be more difficult in our world today. The combination of social mobility, technological innovation, and radical individualism has prioritized personal preference above every other human interest.

In other words, we're becoming more selfish and narcissistic.

We have more options and we've become more accustomed to getting our way than any generation in human history. This has become so common, it fits so neatly with our human nature, that we're not even aware how much our self-interests drive the direction of our lives.

Globalization has created far more mobility in our world; this can be a great benefit for job opportunities and career advancement, but it also makes life less rooted and more transactional.

So many people move to pursue a new job or school opportunity, and every time we move, we leave our network of relationships. Until we find new support and connection, we feel like we're drifting.

Sometimes this means we find "family" in a group of friends. Sometimes we find those relationships with our work colleagues. Technology allows us to create the façade of relationships without many of the benefits.

We have lots of people who know what we're eating, see where we go on vacation, view the latest picture of our family. But we have very few people who are walking with us through some of life's most challenging moments.

We don't have to stop and think about it if we don't want to. From the moment we wake up until we fall asleep, there's no shortage of notification alerts, text messages, on-demand content, to-do lists, emails, and a million other things crying out for our attention.

But the need never goes away.

To satisfy the need, our culture constantly talks about finding "community." Many churches spend time and energy promoting this as one of the primary things they provide.

I appreciate what they're trying to say, but to be honest, it drives me a little crazy. It's vague and nondescript. You can find community in a coffee shop, or the gym, or the guys you play fantasy football with. It just means they're an acquaintance, they know a little bit about you, and you have a few shared interests.

When the Bible talks about spiritual family, I don't think this is what it's talking about. It's not the ability to make casual small talk; it's the people who show up when you need them most.

4. They prioritize personal freedom.

Driven leaders with clear vision and ambition are used to being on their own. They've learned to cope with levels of loneliness. But deep down we all want to know who's with us. We want to know that in the most important moments of life, we won't be alone.

Our rampant consumerism doesn't help us either. We've been trained to look for the best value at the lowest price. Our loyalty in our purchasing is dependent on who will give us the most for the least. This doesn't work in relationships.

You can't be healthy in your relationships if you're always looking for the greatest personal benefit at the lowest cost to yourself. If you treat people like a means to an end, eventually they'll stop trusting you and distance themselves.

I fully understand why people come in and sit on the back row, keep people at a distance, come to church once a month if they don't have other plans, and occasionally watch part of a message online. It's convenient to anonymously slip in and out of church. It fits with a busy life.

But it won't help you when you're going through one of life's big challenges or if you genuinely want to grow.

Those moments require spiritual family.

What's Different About People Who Experience Spiritual Family?

1. They have a big view of God, His Church, and their place in it.

Spiritual family is not a small-minded way to see your church or your friend group as superior or a competition with other lesser environments. It doesn't make you competitive or insecure. It fills you with joy and gratitude. It makes God's Kingdom bigger, not smaller. It motivates you to help everyone else find the place God has for them.

As a church, we give to, encourage, and invest in other churches in our city, our region, and beyond. We see our spiritual family as a part of the larger whole. We don't use it as a cover to critique or criticize other parts of the body of Christ.

At every gathering we have for people who want to learn more about our church, I tell them honestly, "I'd rather have you join Jesus and be placed in another Bible-based church than join our church without a genuine relationship with Him."

Every spiritual family has strengths and weaknesses. They're all different. People often say, "I'm moving to take a job in [a new city]. Do you know of a church like this there?" This always puts me in an awkward position of comparing families.

If I'm close with the person, I try to help them see that their thinking has shaped their decision-making process. The assumption is that the job comes first—it's the hard part—and they can find a church in any city.

I'm not saying God doesn't move people to new places, but they often assume He's behind it without even asking Him. When you have a big view of God, His Church, and your place in it, the spiritual family He places you in is not an afterthought.

2. They believe significant spiritual growth comes on the backside of committing to their spiritual family.

Most people think you find spiritual family after you mature and grow. It's typically the opposite. It's like a marriage. You may have sparks and fireworks when you first meet, while you're dating, and when you're a newlywed. But the real growth, the real development of character, the sanctification and strengthening of the bond, comes from walking together in a committed relationship over time.

None of us can grow when we're constantly reevaluating our commitment level and considering our options. This is true in the classroom, the workplace, the gym, the home, and most definitely in church.

Psychologists call this the paradox of choice. We think having more options is a great freedom, but beyond a small set they end up creating anxiety and dread over whether something better exists somewhere else.

3. They relate to church leadership as pastors, not just teachers.

If you hear this as my idea, we're in trouble. You're going to interpret this as controlling, self-serving, or positional leadership. But if you consider what the Bible says, you may be able to see it from a different perspective.

The apostle Paul told the church in Corinth, "You may have had ten thousand teachers in Christ, but you didn't have many fathers. I became your father in Christ Jesus when I preached the gospel to you" (see 1 Corinthians 4:15). Paul is contrasting spiritual family with classroom education. Some versions translate "teachers" as "mentors," "guides," "guardians," or "instructors."

The Message version says, "There are a lot of people around who can't wait to tell you what you've done wrong, but there aren't many fathers willing to take the time and effort to help you grow up."

Today the body of Christ has exponentially more access to teaching and content than in the rest of Christian history combined. There's never been a time when a Christian could stay home and listen to the greatest preachers in the world from every variety of media available.

And yet your podcast can't pastor you. A pastor is a shepherd—someone who will give an answer for how they cared for the sheep. It's a stewardship.

I'm not asking you to do something I don't do myself. I have a pastor (actually more than one). When I'm coaching or encouraging a pastor, one of the first questions I ask them is, "Who's your pastor?" I'm not looking for more work. I'm checking to see if this leader is living by the same convictions that they expect from the people they're serving. I'm not the only one who lives this way. We have a whole team of pastors and leaders who both receive and give pastoral input because of their confidence in God's pattern of spiritual family.

This is how healthy families work.

4. When challenges come, they lean in instead of stepping back.

When things are going great, it's easy to love everyone and be gracious with others. But when moments of crisis come—and they always do—we get a whole different picture of our lives and relationships.

It's one thing to say you love your church, but when you run into a problem with one of your kids, a small-group leader, or a pastor or staff member, how do you respond?

- Do you wait for more understanding before you react emotionally?
- Do you remain open to the possibility that you don't have all the information?
- Do you allow the history of your relationship and your trust in the relationship to determine how you respond?
- Do you go straight to the person, extend grace and trust, and believe the best about their intentions?

These are high-character ways to respond. They end up strengthening trust, respect, and love. But they're not the only option.

In these moments, some people react so emotionally that they never find out from the person what happened. Others decide what happened unilaterally, only accepting information that supports this view while manipulating and building consensus.

It doesn't have to be this way. It's one thing to say you value honesty in relationships until someone you love and respect honestly tells you something you don't want to hear. This is the character test. But the good news is that you can pass it. And I believe no other environment is as helpful as spiritual family in developing this ability.

This doesn't mean you always agree. It doesn't mean you stay together until Jesus returns. But it does mean you love each other like family— the same way Jesus loves you.

Remember, we first started talking about this idea all the way back in chapter 11, "Where Has God Placed Me?" Because God is the one who does the placing, you know it by conviction and revelation. And this revelation will always be tested.

Sometimes it's your emotions, hurts, or offenses. Sometimes it's an attack from the enemy. Sometimes it's in response to an especially challenging time. But if you are prepared for these tests, you'll be in a much better position to pass them.

Discussion Questions

1. What are some of the different ways to do church? Have you personally experienced them? What did you think?

2. What keeps people from spiritual family? Which of these four challenges was an issue for you? Do you think you've overcome the challenge?

3. How are people who experience spiritual family different? Can you think of a time when you've seen this in action? How did it work?

33

God's Mission

**THE GREAT COMMISSION IS NOT AN OPTION TO BE
CONSIDERED; IT IS A COMMAND TO BE OBEYED.
— J. HUDSON TAYLOR
(FOUNDER OF CHINA INLAND MISSION)**

**EXPECT GREAT THINGS FROM GOD.
ATTEMPT GREAT THINGS FOR GOD.
— WILLIAM CAREY
(FOUNDER OF THE BAPTIST MISSIONARY SOCIETY)**

For the Son of Man came to seek and to save the lost. – Jesus
Luke 19:10

Luke 15 is one of my favorite chapters in the Bible.

Jesus tells three stories in a row: the first about a shepherd with a
hundred sheep who loses one; the second about a woman with ten silver

coins who loses one; and the third about a dad with two sons who—wait for it—loses one.

The third story is often called the Parable of the Prodigal Son. And not only is it one of the most famous stories Jesus told, but it's also one of the most significant stories ever told. Both Charles Dickens and William Shakespeare emphatically made this point. Rembrandt was so moved by the story that it became the inspiration for his most famous work.

These stories give us an incredible window into God's heart. What does God care about? People. When one of them is lost, He doesn't rest until they come home.

I'm not really a dog person, but I love my kids. So, when they came to me and begged for a dog, we ended up with a rescue Golden Retriever named Kingston. He's a good boy, he mostly behaves, and it didn't take long for him to became part of the family.

I'm guessing you know where this is going. When my youngest was a toddler, she'd follow the dog around the house and snuggle with him. So, one day when she couldn't find him, she started to lose it.

The older siblings jumped up and flew off in every direction trying to find him. My wife started making calls and took off in the car. Everyone was so concerned and so determined to find him, they failed to realize our youngest was crying in the front yard all by herself.

As I'm watching this, I have this sudden realization: "My family is on a mission." They were going to do whatever they had to in order to bring this lost member home.

If you have a dog—or worse, if you've lost a child for more than a few minutes—you don't just know what I'm saying; you feel it. This is emotional. This is relational. But this is not what most people think about when they hear the words "evangelism" or "missions."

I've found that most people tend to think of evangelism as a combative debate with people from other belief systems. And, not surprisingly, most people aren't into it.

But whenever I preach this passage from Luke 15, multiple people stop me and ask me to pray for their prodigal. When the person who's lost is a stranger, it's not that important.

When they're family, it's hard to think about anything else. And this is how God thinks about it. He has members of His family lost all over this world, and He wants His kids to be concerned enough to do something about it.

God doesn't need our help to accomplish His purposes, but because He loves us and wants to make us more like Him, He invites us to participate with Him in His mission to redeem the world and bring His lost sons and daughters back home.

This doesn't mean everyone needs to quit their job and go into vocational ministry. That's never been the goal. The job of a pastor isn't to do ministry—that's the responsibility of every Christ-follower. Ephesians 4:11-12 says that Jesus gave some to specific responsibilities in the church to equip the normal, everyday people to do the ministry. That's His strategy.

Think about it: This book you're reading is an expression of this strategy.

NO ONE CAN DO EVERYTHING, BUT EVERYONE CAN DO SOMETHING.

And there's a lot of work to be done. We live in a broken world. The problems and challenges are so great that even the most gifted and godly people in the world can't get the job done on their own.

The job has to get done. It's too important. The church is the only organization in history that exists for its non-members. Churches can get distracted by a lot of other issues that don't have anything to do with reaching the lost.

In Luke 5, Jesus calls four of His most important disciples into His mission: Simon (later Peter) and his brother Andrew, and John and his brother James. They were fishermen. Jesus was teaching and they were cleaning up after fishing all night and catching nothing.

It was probably a little awkward, but Jesus interrupts His message to tell the boys to go right back out and fish. It didn't make sense. It wasn't the time for fishing. These guys were professionals and this carpenter/rabbi was trying to tell them how to do their job. They decide to do it anyway, and when they do, they catch so many fish that their nets start to break and their boats begin to sink.

Jesus is making a point: *I'm not just a preacher. I know how life works. I know more about your work than you do, and if you trust Me, it will transform your life.*

Then He tells them to follow Him because, instead of catching fish, they're now going to catch people.

Here's the point: If you follow Jesus, you catch fish. You don't talk about fish, argue whether or not fish can be caught, maintain the tools to catch fish, or study catching fish.

You go catch them.

Throughout the years, I've found that well-intentioned Christ-followers feel intimidated and reluctant. They worry they don't know enough about the Bible. They're anxious a neighbor or co-worker will ask them a question and they won't have the answer. No one likes to continually participate in activities destined for mediocrity or failure.

The good news is that God's mission is more about *who* you know than *what* you know. Reasonable people don't expect you to have all the answers, but they need to know you care about them. The best thing we can offer someone is the opportunity to experience the love and relationship with God that's changed our life.

The Great Commission ("Go and make disciples") always works best in combination with the Great Commandment ("Love the Lord with all your heart/soul/mind/strength, and love your neighbor as yourself"). Most Christians lean hard in one direction or the other. We need both.

It's certainly true some people are uniquely gifted in evangelism, but I've found that one talented evangelist by themselves can't produce the rich, nuanced, multifaceted image of God that comes from a church committed to the mission of God. No one person can capture the depth and majesty of God's glory. This is why Jesus empowers His Church— His family intentionally filled with an abundance of diverse gifts, personalities, and callings. When people experience this, they say things like, "I can't really explain it but I feel closer to God when I'm there."

To join God in His mission, you don't need expert-level skills, but you do need to be willing to be inconvenienced. People have problems. They require time and energy. But if you're willing to (1) **love** people, (2) **pray** for the lost, (3) **serve** people who are far from God, and (4) **give** generously of your time, talent, and resources, then God will use you in ways that will surprise you.

When a group of people that God has placed together gets really serious about this, they become a fish-catching church. This is exciting because people who catch fish love to tell everyone about it. There's never a shortage of great stories.

But if you're in a fish-catching church, it's also messy. You're probably thinking, *Okay, enough with the metaphor. What does this mean?* Great question. Here's what it looks like practically:

- You're going to have to park farther away.
- You're going to have to show up earlier to find a seat.
- You're going to have to sit next to people who don't look like you and who have different backgrounds.

- You're going to have to build buildings.
- You're not going to have the same small group until Jesus comes back.
- You're going to have to serve people.

These things may inconvenience us, but anything that's healthy is growing, and growth always produces change. We do so much better when we have the right expectations.

Discussion Questions

1. What does God care about? What did Jesus come to do?

2. Whose job is it to "do ministry": the people's or the pastor's?

3. What are four simple ways you can join God in His mission?

Leadership Challenge

— Think of a person in your life who's far from God. It could be a family member, a neighbor, or someone from work or the gym. Think about the different ways you can join God in His mission to reach them.

- Pray for them.
- Invite them to a weekend service.
- Think of a practical way to add value to them.

The Winning Strategy

Discipleship

34

Did Jesus Have a Strategy?

So the word of God spread. The number of disciples in Jerusalem increased rapidly.

Acts 6:7a

If you set out to take over the world, how would you do it? What strategy would you choose?

- Would you build the biggest army?
- Would you take over global media, the internet, and satellite communications?
- Would you control the airports, seaports, railways, and roads?
- Would you attempt to monopolize commerce and market share?

It's not easy—but it can be done.

In the last few centuries, we've seen the Spanish, the British, the Germans, the Russians, the Chinese, and the Americans all achieve some measure of global leadership.

Throughout the course of the Bible, many kings and leaders tried to rule the known world. The Egyptians, the Babylonians, the Persians, and the Romans all managed to do it.

At the height of their power, no one could imagine the world without them. Yet today, these empires only exist in history books.

This phenomenon isn't confined to geopolitics or nation states. We also see it in the business world.

Research shows that 89 percent of the Fortune 500 companies in 1955 no longer exist today.[21] We don't have to go back that far—Circuit City, Blockbuster, America Online, and Kodak were all huge brands in our lifetime and have since vanished.

So, how do we explain the continuing influence of a rabbi from Nazareth who never started a company, never was elected to office, never married or had a family, and died in His early thirties around 2,000 years ago?

Jesus had a very clear strategy. It was a risky move. It was bold. He entrusted the entire future of His mission to the process of discipleship.

All the way back in chapter 12, we learned that Jesus' final words were to go and make disciples. It's often called the Great Commission. It's a co-mission—we do it together. Jesus promised to always be with His followers who went to make disciples of every nation.

We also looked closely at 2 Timothy 2:2 where Paul gave the same charge to a young pastor named Timothy: *What you've heard from me, entrust to faithful people who will train others.*

Jesus could have chosen any number of strategic methods to accomplish His mission. He is God, who became a man and overcame death. More than a Messiah or Savior, He's a risen Lord—the whole world belongs to Him.

And yet, of all the methods at His disposal, Jesus chose to entrust His global expansion project to a group of twelve guys who couldn't be counted on when He needed them the most.

These guys didn't just make mistakes when He was with them. When you read the book of Acts, you realize they were passionate and supremely committed, but they didn't have all the answers. They made major strategic changes all throughout the first fifteen chapters.

They learned on the job.

And before he was the *apostle* Paul, who wrote much of the New Testament and brought the gospel to the rest of the world, he was Saul, a ruthless adversary of Christianity.

DISCIPLESHIP WAS NEVER THE SAFE OPTION, BUT THERE'S NO DENYING IT'S WHAT JESUS WANTED. AND IT'S STILL WHAT HE'S AFTER TODAY.

When we hear the word "disciple," most people think of a classroom or a small-group setting where participants study information. The emphasis is on teaching and spiritual content. Some people may imagine Jesus' earliest followers, and still others don't have any context for what it means.

Simply put, discipleship is one Christ-follower helping another take their next step. It's relational. It's *watch what I do*, then *you do it*, then *we talk about how we can do it better.*

A disciple is more than a student trying to gain information; it's a committed apprentice growing in aptitude and ability.

You won't experience this with a half-hearted commitment. You can't get it from a class. You have to commit to it as a lifestyle. But once you do, you won't want to go back.

Discipleship is caught more than it's taught. You just start taking steps. It's kind of like a coaching tree in the NFL.

You can watch every game and memorize statistics, but if you want to become a coach in the NFL, you need to spend time around the people who are actually doing it.

In the 2018 NFL playoffs, all twelve of the head coaches could be traced back to the leadership of Bill Walsh or Bill Parcells. In other words, every one of these men learned how to lead men and coach football on a team whose culture was shaped by either Walsh or Parcells.

Some of these coaches started as unpaid volunteers who shagged balls or as technicians in the film room. They just started taking steps and became a part of the team.

Parcells hasn't coached a game since 2006, and Walsh passed away in 2007. Yet, their influence endures. It hasn't slowed down over time; the impact has only grown.

Bill Walsh was an assistant for the Cincinnati Bengals and applied for the head coaching job in 1976. When he wasn't chosen, he made a commitment that when he did become a head coach, he would do everything he could to help his assistants become head coaches themselves.

In 1979, he was hired as the head coach of the San Francisco 49ers, where he won the Super Bowl in '81, '84, and '88. The last championship was especially meaningful because it came against the Bengals—who are still looking for their first Super Bowl victory.

What's even more remarkable has been the success of the apprentices of these two coaches. Six different head coaching descendants of Walsh and three from Parcells have hoisted the Lombardi Trophy. In the past 40 years, only seven times has a team won the Super Bowl *without* a connection to Walsh or Parcells.

Football is only a game, but this demonstrates the power of the discipleship process.

When I was a young pastor, I read a little book called *The Master Plan of Evangelism*. It simply and clearly outlined the intentional brilliance of Jesus' strategy. It changed the way I thought about ministry.

Out of all the strategies available to Jesus, the author Robert Coleman properly and succinctly clarifies His plan: "Men were to be his method of winning the world to God."[22]

Jesus didn't bank on miracles. He didn't prioritize big events. He didn't focus on branding and marketing. He didn't cater to influencing the rich, the famous, or the powerful. He didn't fix all the social problems of the day. Each of these were accomplished along the way, but they weren't the method.

He made disciples who would make disciples who would make disciples, *ad infinitum*, until the whole world has the chance to be His disciple.

This is not the fastest or most exciting strategy. It's the long play.

> Here is where we must begin just like Jesus. It will be slow, tedious, painful, and probably unnoticed by people at first, but the end result will be glorious, even if we don't live to see it. Seen this way, though, it becomes a big decision in the ministry.
>
> We must decide where we want our ministry to count—in the momentary applause of popular recognition or in the reproduction of our lives in a few chosen people who will carry on our work faithfully long after we are gone. Really it is a question of which generation we are living for.[23]

You're probably thinking, *Slow, tedious, painful, and probably unnoticed—where do I sign up?!*

While it may be these things, it's also the way to create a movement capable of spanning generations, cultures, languages, and thousands of years. There's more momentum in the mission of Jesus today than when He started it.

That's the power of discipleship.

Discussion Questions

1. What was Jesus' mission? What was His strategy? Was this a risky choice? Explain.

2. Is discipleship more like being a student or an apprentice? What's the difference?

3. How can an NFL coaching tree be like the process of discipleship?

4. Are you a disciple of Jesus? How do you know?

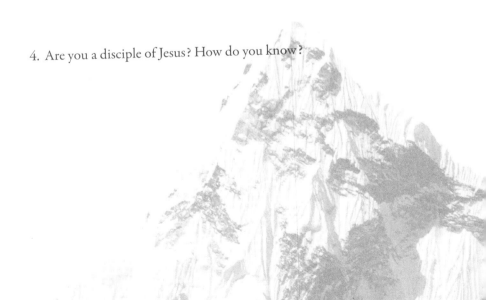

35

How Does Discipleship Work?

Part One

*This is how we know we are in him: Whoever claims
to live in him must live as Jesus did.*
1 John 2:5b-6 NIV

*For I have given you an example, that you should
do as I have done to you.* – Jesus
John 13:15 NKJV

*And He appointed twelve, so that they would be with
Him and that He could send them out to preach.*
Mark 3:14 NASB

Out of all the strategies available to Him, Jesus prioritized discipleship. And through this process, billions of people, over thousands of years, have come into a relationship with Jesus and have advanced His mission throughout the earth.

You're reading these words because His mission has been a success.

If discipleship is more than a class, if it's more than the exchange of spiritual information, how does it work?

Before we can jump to how we give it to others—which is a big part of the process—it's important for us to understand what it means to receive this kind of discipleship coaching.

First, it's a commitment to ongoing relationships with both Jesus and the people He calls you to. Mark 3:14 shows us that Jesus appointed the twelve to be *with Him*. This is no small thing. You won't become like people you aren't with.

Coleman describes Jesus' approach this way: "He did not ask anyone to do or be anything which first he had not demonstrated in his own life, thereby not only proving its workability, but also its relevance to his mission."[24]

Discipleship happens along the way in day-to-day life. It's far more about a demonstration than an explanation. You have to see it in action. It's more "show me" than "tell me."

This doesn't mean you spend your life at the church or you don't have other relationships. It's different from a personal advisor who approves all your decisions, a personal priest who spiritualizes every issue, or a friend who encourages you no matter what choice you make.

Someone who "disciples" you models for you what it looks like to follow Jesus in the essential areas of life and then challenges you to do the same.

This is only possible when the apprentice commits to prioritize the relationship and faithfully continues to grow. This means you believe that God is working in you, He wants you to grow, and He's going to help you.

In other words, you have to be faithful.

Second, it's a commitment to easily identifiable growth. You're not going to be like Jesus overnight. But when you're committed to the process, you end up becoming more and more like Him.

If you're always around but you're never maturing or growing, then something is off. This doesn't mean you're perfect, but there should be clear signs of progress.

- Are you reading your Bible and growing in your understanding of God's Word?
- Are you experiencing God's presence through your prayer life and times of worship?
- Are you passing the character test? How would the people closest to you describe your relationships? Are you hard to offend? Do you forgive quickly? Do you believe the best about people?
- Are you leading and serving your wife the way Jesus leads the church?
- Are you training your children and developing them?
- Are you reproducing what God's doing in you in someone else?

The specifics of these look different for everyone, but these things are constantly happening in the life of a disciple. None of these things are reserved for a select few professional Christians. These things can be your normal, everyday life.

No guy likes to admit he doesn't know how to do things. We like pro tips, life hacks, and do-it-yourself because it makes us feel like we know more than we actually do.

The bottom line is, if you're gaining a bunch of spiritual information but the relationships you care the most about are unhealthy and unspiritual, then you're not winning in the process of discipleship.

Discipleship provides the context to observe what these relationships can look like. As a result, this calls each of us to a new standard in our own development.

We won't accomplish any of these things by accident. We have to be intentional. We need a clear plan. And we need relationships in our lives to help us get there.

Finally, it's a commitment to receive coaching with the right heart. A disciple is teachable. They're not arrogant or disrespectful. They posture themselves as learners. They're quick to take responsibility. They're grateful for correction instead of being defensive.

Coleman describes it this way: "Jesus did not have the time nor the desire to scatter himself on those who wanted to make their own terms of discipleship. Hence it was that a would-be disciple was made to count the cost."[25]

They're coachable.

We've all seen highlights of the player who snaps at his coach—it seems more common today than ever before. It's never a good sign, and in a healthy situation, it means the player's headed for the bench until he gets his attitude right.

This doesn't mean you can't ask questions or disagree, but it does impact how you communicate. Winning teams don't undermine the coach in the middle of the game—even when they disagree. They put the interests of the team ahead of their personal preferences. They realize they may not have all the information. They're capable of communicating their opinion in the appropriate moment.

HOW YOU HANDLE CONFLICT REVEALS A GREAT DEAL ABOUT YOUR LEVEL OF MATURITY. IT'S A TRUST ISSUE.

Do you believe the coach wants the best for you? More importantly, do you believe God does?

Jesus loves us so much that He leads us right into these situations to help us see what's in our heart. Remember the character test? It's easy to think you're self-controlled, mature, and humble until you get challenged.

You can't have an impact without a collision. We don't know whether we trust our relationships until our will gets crossed. The immature man receives correction as rejection. The wise and mature man receives correction with a humble, open heart.

The immature man looks for an out when he gets challenged. He wants to get traded to a new team. He starts looking for a new coach. The mature man realizes he doesn't change coaches in the middle of the game.

The Bible says that you find out whether someone is a mocker or a wise man when you correct them (see Proverbs 9:8-9; 17:10).

The truth is, correction is typically a small part of the recipe. The percentage of instruction and encouragement far outweighs the discipline, but I've never met a healthy man who's incapable of receiving discipline. I've seen many incredibly talented men who never reached their potential because they were unwilling to embrace the process.

When a man bristles at healthy correction, his relationships suffer—especially in the areas of his life he cares about the most. It holds him back in the workplace, undermines him in his home, and limits his friendships.

Discussion Questions

1. Is discipleship more about an explanation or a demonstration? Why does this matter? How does this change the way we grow in the process?

2. Name two of the six easily identifiable signs of growth in the life of a disciple. Which of these six are growing in your life?

3. What does it mean to be coachable? What makes this hard for us? How does this impact our relationships?

36

How Does Discipleship Work?

Part Two

You didn't choose me. I chose you. I appointed you to go and produce lasting fruit. – Jesus
John 15:16a NLT

Preach the word; be prepared in season and out of season; correct, rebuke and encourage—with great patience and careful instruction.
2 Timothy 4:2 NIV

Before He ascended to heaven, Jesus told His disciples to go and make disciples. Why did He make such a big deal out of this?

He knew that disciples don't make themselves. He spent three years with these twelve men—challenging their mindsets, building their faith, developing their leadership, confronting their selfishness and immaturity, and inspiring them to become everything God created them to be.

More than investing in these particular men for their specific role in the mission, Jesus was establishing a model for all of His followers, at all times and in all places.

In the last chapter, we took a careful look at this process and how you can tell if you're a disciple. **Now we turn our attention to the practical details of how you make disciples.**

It takes a disciple to make a disciple. Technically, you're not a disciple until you make a disciple.

YOU TEACH WHAT YOU KNOW; YOU REPRODUCE WHAT YOU ARE.

Remember, discipleship is not a function of personality or personal preference. Disciples aren't clones. We don't make them look like us; we help them become who Jesus created them to be. If we're only pointing people to our way of life, we're doing it wrong.

All of us become like the people we spend time with and the ideas we believe. Coleman explains it this way:

> The world is desperately seeking someone to follow. That they will follow someone is certain, but will that person be one who knows the way of Christ, or will he or she be one like themselves leading them only on into greater darkness? This is the decisive question of our plan of life.[26]

Jesus' entire strategy hinges on men and women being willing to become disciples who make disciples. We learned that when a disciple commits to Jesus and the process of discipleship, they commit to easily identifiable growth, and they commit to receive coaching with a right attitude.

If this is what it means to be one, how do you make one? You have to start with finding a candidate.

When people first get excited about discipleship, they ask me, "Where do you find one?" If you're a dad, the best place to look is in your own home. The most important disciples you'll ever make live under your roof. You don't just raise your children; you train them.

You can't force your kids to be disciples, but it's your responsibility to inspire and invite them into the process. It's not good stewardship to invest your time and energy into others at the expense of the people for whom you're already responsible.

But what about those outside your home?

In Jesus' day, crowds of people would follow behind the most respected rabbis, waiting to be selected. When the rabbi was ready, he would stop and select his disciple. Jesus flipped this tradition upside down. He went and found fishermen, tax collectors, scholars, and radical nationalists and called them to follow Him.

Jesus didn't pick people wandering around Nazareth with nothing to do. The people He called were busy with the everyday responsibilities of life—running a business, taking care of their family, etc. But He saw in each of them a measure of leadership, the capacity to commit to something bigger than themselves, and a willingness to grow.

How do you know what to look for?

It's the same way for us today: The person you're looking for is not necessarily waiting for something because they have nothing better to do. They have responsibility, some sense of direction and vision, and a hunger and a desire to grow in their relationship with God and the process to become the person God created them to be.

Your confidence in your ability to call them to this process comes from your conviction to the process yourself. If you're going to be effective, you have to believe God chose you for the task and is going to help you in the process. This holds true whether you're talking about your kids or someone else. There will be plenty of opportunities for you to be offended or to feel rejection. If your commitment is only as strong as the approval of others, you will struggle.

When you realize you're doing this for Jesus, to advance His Kingdom, and to serve the person, you will be willing to keep working the process before you see the clear evidence of good fruit.

Once you find them, what do you do?

As Paul told Timothy, you have to be ready when it's convenient and when it's not. You start with the Word—this means you start with what God's Word says, not your personal opinion or common sense. What separates discipleship from personal coaching or traditional mentoring are the authority and power that come from the Word.

Here's Coleman again: "It is not better methods, but better men and women who know their Redeemer from personal experience . . . who see his vision and feel his passion for the world . . . who are willing to be nothing so that he might be everything."[27]

If their attitudes or behavior don't line up with the Word, help them to see this. Their conflict is not with you—it's with what God says.

Your role is to encourage, coach, and support them through the process as someone who cares for them and wants the best.

YOUR HOPE FOR THEIR GROWTH IS NOT IN YOUR ABILITY TO PERSUADE THEM OR SOUND SMART. YOUR GOAL IS TO HELP THEM HEAR GOD AND OBEY.

And like Paul coached Timothy, you have to be ready to correct, to rebuke, but mostly to encourage with great patience and careful instruction. There will be times when you will feel like you're saying the same thing over and over. It's okay. That's how people feel about helping you. It's part of the process.

Listen carefully, be self-aware, and choose your words intentionally so that you give the person every opportunity for clear understanding. If you don't know what to say, tell them. Let them know you're going to look into it, pray about it, and get back to them.

Hold them to a high standard. Keep calling them back to their commitment to prioritize their relationship with Jesus, to demonstrate clear growth, and to receive coaching with a right heart. If they ignore you, call them on it. If they didn't listen to what you talked about last time, don't give them a pass and move on to something else.

At the risk of repeating myself, I want to make sure you get this. I don't want anyone to feel stuck or unprepared. So, in closing, here's a simple summary.

How Do You Make a Disciple?

1. Get someone.
Look first in your home. Then look in the places you're already spending time (work, church, small group, hobbies, etc.). Ask God to show you and be clear on what you're asking of them. Remember, it's relationship-based, not a class or a program.

2. Be with them.
It won't work if you don't spend time with them. Giving someone your time is one of the greatest expressions of value and love we can offer. In John 3:22, Jesus went out to the countryside to spend time with His disciples. Attitudes, perspectives, and character issues only surface when you're around people. You can do this in a small group over a meal; you can do it one on one while you're enjoying a hobby; you can

do it in a conference room at work—you just need time together and a commitment to the process.

3. Help them in the basics.

You begin at the beginning. Help them understand what it means to have a relationship with God. Help them learn to read the Bible themselves. Help them develop a prayer life. Lead them through the foundations materials you went through in this book (Section 2).

4. Challenge and encourage them.

We don't grow in our comfort zone; we need a coach to motivate and inspire us to become more. Men want to win, but we get frustrated when we don't know how. We need someone to show us. Help them identify and move toward their next step. This is what discipleship is all about. This recipe always includes a mix of encouragement, understanding, patience, and the occasional confrontation.

Be interested in their lives. Don't just make small talk. Ask them how they're doing and listen. Ask a follow-up question. Make it easy for them to be honest with you and to process how they're doing. This requires time and trust. Text them and encourage them when they have a big meeting at work or they're going through something with their family. Remember, this is more than the exchange of information. It's relational.

You have everything you need to get out there and make a disciple.

Discussion Questions

1. What does it take to make a disciple? What's the difference between what you teach and what you reproduce?

2. Where is the first place you should look to find a disciple? Can you force your kids to be disciples?

3. What makes someone a good candidate for discipleship? Do you think you embody these traits?

4. What do you start with in the discipleship relationship? What is your role? Have you done this yet? How can you get better at this?

37

Lasting Legacy

Lord, what are human beings that you care for them,
mere mortals that you think of them? They are like
a breath; their days are like a fleeting shadow.
Psalm 144:3-4 NIV

One generation shall commend your works to another,
and shall declare your mighty acts.
Psalm 145:4 ESV

I have fought the good fight, I have finished the race,
I have kept the faith.
2 Timothy 4:7 ESV

In the first part of our journey, we talked about the idea of legacy. I believe it's important to come back to this concept again.

Bill Walsh and Bill Parcells were Super Bowl champions. But what makes them so remarkable is more than the victories and trophies they won; it's the success of those who came after them. Collectively, their disciples achieved more over a longer period of time than either of them did as a head coach.

This is the way to win. This is an enduring legacy.

Parcells retired in 2006, and Walsh passed away in 2007. Some of the teams have relocated. More than a few of the teams play in different stadiums. Many of the rules have been changed.

Only two NFL coaches from that season are still leading their franchises: Sean Payton of the New Orleans Saints, and Bill Belichick of the New England Patriots. Both of them were mentored by Parcells and both of them are Super Bowl champions.

This is the power of legacy. Instead of weakening, its influence grows stronger over time. As inspiring as this may be, it's only football. It's a bunch of grown men tackling each other to carry a ball across a line. It's a game.

A life focused on the championships and records compiled by one person is small. Life is short. Mansions, kingdoms, and even the great wonders of the world fade.

You can't take your trophies. You can't take your titles or promotions. You can't take your favorite car. You can't take your house.

THE ONLY THING THAT ENDURES IS THE IMPACT WE MAKE ON PEOPLE, WHO GO ON TO INFLUENCE OTHERS.

In a social media world, it can be easy to forget that what we really care about are not likes from strangers—what we really want are the love and approval of those closest to us.

No single individual has had more of an impact on the lives of people than Jesus. Bible scholars believe He lived no longer than 35 years. Today, roughly 2,000 years after His death, more than two billion people around the world claim to have a meaningful relationship with Him.

This has been Jesus' legacy from the very beginning. His Church was built on the commitment and sacrifice of His closest followers. They believed in Him so deeply that they were willing—and even grateful—to give their lives for the cause.

His mother believed He was more than her son. She believed He was the Son of God, the risen Lord, and the Savior of the world. His younger brother struggled with this initially but became so convinced that he served in a leadership role in the early church, wrote a significant book in the New Testament, and laid down his life not out of family loyalty but out of deep obedience to the King of kings.

All but one of Jesus' closest friends overcame imprisonment, persecution, and every kind of adversity to make disciples, plant churches, and reach the known world with the gospel.

No other person in history even comes close to this standard.

If we're in Christ, we're a part of this legacy—not as rivals or competition to His influence, but heirs of the promise. This promise includes healthy relationships and a legacy big enough to outlive us.

I've had the privilege to walk with men and women of character whom I respect deeply through the last days of their lives. It's been my honor to share in these moments with my friends and family.

None of them ever asked to see their 401k statement in their final hours. They wanted to hold the hands of the people they loved. They wanted to know that the impact of their lives would live beyond them.

The concept of legacy is real to me. My dad's legacy is complete. The moments we spent celebrating his life were unforgettable. When a man runs his race well, the finish line is a holy moment. You sense God's pleasure.

My dad's last years were the best years of his life. He was never the kind of person who was into the latest trend or the targets cultural experts defined. He knew what he valued, and down the home stretch he became even more intentional. He added value to every close relationship in his life.

It was so inspiring to all of us who walked with him. It changed the way we think about our legacy. I always respected my dad and appreciated his values. Even in our final moments together, I was overcome with the realization of the incomparable impact he made in the lives of those he loved the most. He inspired me to follow his example.

YOU'LL NEVER REGRET THE WISE CHOICES YOU MAKE TO PRIORITIZE WHAT JESUS VALUES.

Remember, discipleship was Jesus' method and His mission was His Church. It's the one thing He promised to build. He made disciples to advance His mission through His Church. We call this spiritual family. In the end, our legacy will be our commitment to spiritual family and discipleship. It will be the people we influence who love and serve the mission of Jesus. It rises and falls on our ability to transfer these values to the next generation.

Nothing else we invest in will come close to this.

Whether or not they play golf, most men don't take time to think about legacy until they're on the back nine of life. This is a mistake. Every one of us has an expiration date. We don't know when it's coming—but it's coming.

When you're in Christ, you don't fear death. You live with the hope of the promise of glory. Your eternal future is secure, and you live with the expectation of spending forever with a perfect God who loves you completely.

This shouldn't be a cop-out, rendering what happens now inconsequential. Instead, this should be a sober reminder of the fleeting nature of this life. We only get one shot. We have a responsibility to make the most of it as a gift to the Lord.

Discipleship is slow and tedious, but in the end, it's glorious. Usually, you can't tell how deeply significant it is in the moment. But when you experience the fruit of it, there's nothing like it. The relationships you form through this process become your legacy.

There's no greater investment you can make than your relationships. You don't want to leave anything unresolved. Don't put it off. Don't find a reason why another time would be better.

- Forgive quickly and freely.
- Work through offenses.
- Don't prioritize your personal agendas over people.
- Help someone else accomplish their dreams.
- Be generous with honor and respect.
- Tell people how much you care about them.
- Leave an inheritance for the people closest to you in the things they care about most.

If you choose to live this way now, your legacy will far exceed your wildest ambitions. And it will continue to grow long after you're gone.

Discussion Questions

1. Are there issues you've been putting off? Are you carrying unforgiveness toward anyone? What's holding you back from dealing with it?

2. Are there things unsaid in the relationships you care about? You can't fix it by yourself, but what can you do to help it get healthy?

3. What do you want your funeral to look like? What are you doing now to make this possible?

38

What Do We Do Now?

I press on toward the goal to win the prize for which God
has called me heavenward in Christ Jesus.
Philippians 3:14

We've come to the end of this part of the journey. In sports, it's like the end of the season. In school, it's like the end of the semester. Starting is different from finishing. The middle of the season is a grind; the end is a whole range of emotions.

You should feel great for making this investment in your future and sticking with it to the end. I trust you've learned something, and if you've implemented what you've learned, then you're already seeing results in your life and relationships.

But here's the problem we face when we experience these exciting new growth steps: We all have the tendency to underestimate the involvement of others in our development.

It's like the unheralded athlete who works really hard and surprises everyone by making the roster. He's hungry, he's coachable, and he's putting in the work. When the moment comes, he's ready and he makes an impact on the game and helps the team win.

The fans and the media start to see him differently. People are paying attention.

Now the story comes to an inevitable fork in the road:

- When the person is mature, they understand how their success was the result of the efforts of many people, continue to work hard and develop their character, and go on to a long, successful career.

- When a person is immature, they give themselves all the credit, leave to go to the team that will pay them the most money as fast as possible, lose the process that caused their growth, and squander their potential.

We see it happen all the time. We want to make sure you have the greatest opportunity for success moving forward.

It's easy to think, *I've got this. I've learned so much. And I have the book if I need a little refresher.* Remember how we started: This is less about getting information and more about a process designed to help you win. The structure, the coaching, the relationships, the support—they're all a big part of the recipe.

It's the way to win.

As Paul wrote to the people of Philippi, God has set up a clear goal—a prize like a victory medal or a championship ring. The ultimate winner, our great champion, is Jesus. And if we want to win, we have to keep pressing forward to live like He lived.

Jesus led His team with clear communication. He prepared them for transitions: when He started His ministry, when they started to draw crowds, when they went to Jerusalem and met resistance, when they approached the time of His death, after His resurrection, and before He ascended to heaven.

In each of these situations, He prepared them by reminding them to stay connected to God, to each other, and to the people they were serving.

He knew they needed to be reminded. We all do.

If you're reading this book by yourself, these concepts can change your life. But in order to live them out, you need to lean into relationships. If you're reading this book with a group, the weekly gathering part of this process is coming to a close. But in order for the growth to continue, the relationships must endure. This will only happen if you're intentional. When you have a regularly scheduled meeting, it's easy to think you're more connected than you are.

It's far too common for guys to look up after a couple of weeks, a couple of months, even a year, and think, *Where did everyone go?* When this happens, in any area of our lives, most of us revert back to patterns and habits that are less than ideal.

Don't make the common mistake of thinking, *I've been really committed. I'm going to take a break for a little bit and then I'll get back into it.* There's nothing wrong with taking a short break—as long as you have a clear plan with a target date to get back to your winning ways.

Vince Lombardi famously said, "Winning is not a sometime thing. It's an all-the-time thing. You don't do things right once in a while; you do them right all the time."[28]

The thing that separates a championship team from a dynasty is that the former experiences a moment of greatness while the latter sustains greatness over a long period of time.

Stay close to things that have helped you learn how to win.

- Keep challenging and encouraging other men around you—pray for them, send them a text, and find ways to continue to strengthen each other.

- Keep leading your family to engage and serve at church.
- Keep prioritizing your Bible and spending time with God.
- Keep serving and developing your wife and children.
- Engage in the life of your church and use your gifts to make a difference.
- Make disciples.

I've noticed that when men go back to focusing on their own projects and needs, they get isolated because they have a fairly established routine to manage their daily lives.

But when they really make it a goal to do the things listed above, they quickly realize that their willpower and structure aren't enough to get it done. They need the help of other men.

Talented people achieve goals and set records—it takes a team to win.

That's why God gives us His team, His Church. There's nothing like it. It provides the clear path for development (discipleship) in the context of committed, trusting relationships (spiritual family).

My life's goal has always been to help people win. I think about it every morning when I wake up. It's how God made me. If there's one thing I want you to take away, it's the simple confidence to know that by the grace of God you can do this.

It's not unattainable. It's not impossible. It doesn't matter how you were raised, how old you are, or the mistakes you've made in your past. None of those things can disqualify you if you keep showing up with a coachable attitude and a willingness to get better.

You can win.

I'm proud of the steps you've taken. God wants you on His team. Let's keep winning together!

Discussion Questions

1. How are you going to carry the relationships you've made during this time forward?

2. What's your next step in leading your family?

3. What's your next step in making a disciple?

NOTES

---

1   Vince Lombardi, "What It Takes to Be Number One," http:/www.vincelombardi.com/number-one.html.

2   See the groundbreaking book on the subject, *Mindset: The New Psychology of Success*, by Carol Dweck.

3   Romans 12:1-2; Ephesians 4:22-24; Colossians 2:6-7

4   Tim Ferriss, https://www.brainyquote.com/quotes/tim_ferriss_529031.

5   Neil Howe, "America, the Sleep Deprived," Forbes Magazine, https://www.forbes.com/sites/neilhowe/2017/08/18/america-the-sleep-deprived/#6c1709d81a38.

6   Proverbs 14:23

7   Exodus 20:8-11

8   Romans 5:8-10; 8:32

9   Ruth 1:16-17

10 John 15:9-17

11 John 19:26-27

12 Stephen Marche, "Is Facebook Making Us Lonely?" The Atlantic, https://www.theatlantic.com/magazine/archive/2012/05/is-facebook-making-us-lonely/308930/.

13 Liz Mineo, "Good Genes Are Nice but Joy Is Better," The Harvard Gazette, https://news.harvard.edu/gazette/story/2017/04/over-nearly-80-years-harvard-study-has-been-showing-how-to-live-a-healthy-and-happy-life/.

14 Maria Bouselli, "More Couples Want to Be Roomies Before Walking Down the Aisle," The Knot, https://www.theknot.com/content/more-couples-living-together-before-marriage.

15 Meilan Solly, "U.S. Life Expectancy Drop for Third Year in a Row, Reflecting Rising Drug Overdoses, Suicides," Smithsonian Magazine, https://www.smithsonianmag.com/smart-news/us-life-expectancy-drops-third-year-row-reflecting-rising-drug-overdose-suicide-rates-180970942/.

16 Henry Cloud, *Boundaries for Leaders* (New York, NY: Harper Collins Publishers, 2013), p. 14.

17 Simon Sinek, *Together Is Better* (New York, NY: Penguin Random House LLC, 2016), p. 66.

18 Matthew 21:42; Mark 12:10; Luke 20:17

19 1 Corinthians 15:12-19

20 Dale Carnegie, *How to Win Friends and Influence People* (New York, NY: Simon & Schuster, 2009).

21 Mark J. Perry, "Fortune 500 firms 1955 v. 2017: Only 60 remain thanks to the creative destruction that fuels economic prosperity," https://www.aei.org/carpe-diem/fortune-500-firms-1955-v-2017-only-12-remain-thanks-to-the-creative-destruction-that-fuels-economic-prosperity/.

22 Robert Coleman, *The Master Plan of Evangelism* (Grand Rapids, MI: Bake Publishing Group, 1963), p. 21.

23 Ibid., p. 35.

24 Ibid., p. 77.

25 Ibid., p. 52.

26 Ibid., p. 121.

27 Ibid., p. 109.

28 Vince Lombardi, "What It Takes to Be Number One," http://www.vincelombardi.com/number-one.html.

ANSWER KEY

CHAPTER SIX
1. Dead
2. All of us
3. Nature—even our desires and thoughts are sinful.
4. God makes us alive with Christ.
5. The gift of God

CHAPTER SEVEN
1. Their sin—and our sin—sent Jesus to the cross.
2. They were cut to the heart; it was more than information—it moved them to action.
3. Repent and be baptized—every one of you—in the name of Jesus Christ for the forgiveness of sins.
4. You, your children, all who are far off, as many as the Lord our God will call!

CHAPTER EIGHT
1. They do what He says.
2. Put them into practice.
3. They *both* did.
4. Both heard and knew the words—only one put them into practice.

CHAPTER NINE
1. Laws, statutes, precepts, commands, decrees
2. Perfect and revives the soul; trustworthy and makes the simple wise
3. Joy to the heart and light to the eyes
4. More precious than gold, sweeter than honey
5. These laws warn God's servant and give great rewards to those who keep them.
6. Our words and our thoughts please God.

CHAPTER TEN
1. An advocate—another name for a lawyer, representative, counsel
2. Helps us and is with us forever
3. The Spirit of truth
4. The world does not accept Him because they can't see Him and they don't know Him.

5. He lives *with* us and He is *in* us.
6. Teach us all things and remind us of everything He has said
7. Helps us understand; reminds us after we've read/heard the Word

CHAPTER ELEVEN
1. Teaching, fellowship, breaking of bread, and prayer
2. Awe from the many signs and wonders; they couldn't believe what God was doing.
3. Everyone was together and gave to those in need.
4. They met together and were filled with glad and sincere hearts.
5. They had favor with God and man and the Lord added to their number daily people being saved.

CHAPTER TWELVE
1. Be strong in grace—this process requires strength that only comes as a gift from God
2. Things Paul told him in the presence of many witnesses
3. Reliable people able/qualified to help others
4. Paul, Timothy, reliable people, others (no less than 4)
5. Soldier—under authority; athlete—plays by the rules; farmer—works hard and knows how to receive. All three require you to be able to do it, not simply know information about it.

VISIT US ONLINE

MILESTONECHURCH.COM

ALSO FROM JEFF LITTLE

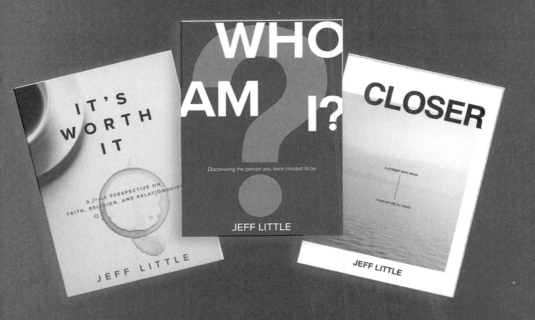

FOR MORE INFO OR TO PURCHASE,
VISIT MILESTONERESOURCES.COM.

CONNECT WITH JEFF LITTLE

📷 **@JEFFLITTLE**

🐦 **@JEFF_LITTLE**

📘 **@PASTORJEFFLITTLE**